READING/WRITING
COMPANION

Mc
Graw
Hill

COVER: James Haskins

mheducation.com/prek-12

Send all inquiries to:
McGraw-Hill Education
Two Penn Plaza
New York, New York 10121

ISBN: 978-0-07-700889-5
MHID: 0-07-700889-8

Printed in the United States of America.

9 10 LMN 24 23

B

Welcome to Wonders !

Read exciting **Literature, Science,** and **Social Studies** texts!

★ **LEARN** about the world around you!

★ **THINK, SPEAK,** and **WRITE** about genres!

★ **COLLABORATE** in discussion and inquiry!

★ **EXPRESS** yourself!

my.mheducation.com
Use your student login to read core texts, practice grammar and spelling, explore research projects and more!

UNIT 1

GENRE STUDY 1 NARRATIVE NONFICTION

Essential Question 1
SHARED READ "The Monster in the Mountain" 2
Vocabulary/Metaphors and Similes 6
Reread 8
Maps and Models 9
Main Idea and Key Details 10
WRITING Respond to Reading 12
Research and Inquiry 13
ANCHOR TEXT Analyze *Into the Volcano* 14
WRITING Respond to Reading 17
PAIRED SELECTION Analyze "Donna O'Meara: The Volcano Lady" ... 18
Author's Craft: Print and Graphic Features 21
Text Connections/Research and Inquiry 22
WRITING Personal Narrative 24

GENRE STUDY 2 REALISTIC FICTION

Essential Question 32
SHARED READ "Cow Music" 34
Vocabulary/Context Clues 38
Visualize 40
Narrator and Dialogue 41
Character, Setting, Plot 42
WRITING Respond to Reading 44
Research and Inquiry 45
ANCHOR TEXT Analyze *Little Blog on the Prairie* .. 46
WRITING Respond to Reading 49
PAIRED SELECTION Analyze "The Writing on the Wall" ... 50
Author's Craft: Imagery 53
Text Connections/Research and Inquiry 54

GENRE STUDY 3 ARGUMENTATIVE TEXT

Essential Question.. 56
SHARED READ TIME "Making Money: A Story of Change"............. 58
Vocabulary/Root Words.. 62
Reread... 64
Graphs and Sidebars.. 65
Author's Point of View... 66
WRITING Respond to Reading.. 68
Research and Inquiry... 69
ANCHOR TEXT Analyze *The Economic Roller Coaster*................. 70
WRITING Respond to Reading.. 72
PAIRED SELECTION Analyze "Our Federal Reserve at Work"............ 73
Author's Craft: Cause and Effect................................... 75
Text Connections/Accuracy and Rate................................. 76
WRITING Opinion Essay... 78

WRAP UP THE UNIT

SHOW WHAT YOU LEARNED
- Argumentative Text: "Allowances for Kids: The Great Debate"........ 86
- Realistic Fiction: "Not So Bad After All"......................... 89

EXTEND YOUR LEARNING
- Comparing Genres.. 92
- Word Origins... 93
- Connect to Content... 94

TRACK YOUR PROGRESS
- What Did You Learn?... 96

Research and Inquiry... 97

Digital Tools Find this eBook and other resources at **my.mheducation.com**

GENRE STUDY 1 **EXPOSITORY TEXT**

Essential Question 98
SHARED READ "The Democracy Debate" 100
Vocabulary/Greek and Latin Prefixes 104
Ask and Answer Questions 106
Charts and Diagrams 107
Compare and Contrast 108
WRITING Respond to Reading 110
Research and Inquiry 111
ANCHOR TEXT Analyze *Who Created Democracy?* 112
WRITING Respond to Reading 115
PAIRED SELECTION Analyze "How Ideas Become Laws" 116
Author's Craft: Author's Purpose 119
Text Connections/Research and Inquiry 120
WRITING Expository Essay 122

GENRE STUDY 2 **HISTORICAL FICTION**

Essential Question 130
SHARED READ "Yaskul's Mighty Trade" 132
Vocabulary/Connotations and Denotations 136
Make Predictions 138
Setting and Foreign Language Words 139
Point of View 140
WRITING Respond to Reading 142
Research and Inquiry 143
ANCHOR TEXT Analyze *Roman Diary* 144
WRITING Respond to Reading 147
PAIRED SELECTION Analyze "The Genius of Roman Aqueducts" 148
Author's Craft: Author's Purpose 151
Text Connections/Research and Inquiry 152

GENRE STUDY 3 POETRY

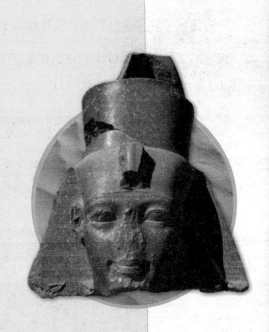

Essential Question.. 154

SHARED READ "Ozymandias".................................. 156

Vocabulary/Personification.................................. 160

Rhyme Scheme and Meter.................................... 162

Sonnet and Lyric Poetry....................................... 163

Theme.. 164

WRITING Respond to Reading............................. 166

Research and Inquiry... 167

ANCHOR TEXT Analyze "Majestic"..................... 168

WRITING Respond to Reading............................. 170

PAIRED SELECTION Analyze "Maestro"............... 171

Author's Craft: Word Choice................................ 173

Text Connections/Expression and Phrasing... 174

WRITING Lyric Poem.. 176

WRAP UP THE UNIT

SHOW WHAT YOU LEARNED
- Expository Text: "The Roots of Democracy?"............ 184
- Poetry: "The Canyon"... 187

EXTEND YOUR LEARNING
- Onomatopoeia/Suffixes.. 190
- Historical and Cultural Setting............................ 191
- Connect to Content.. 192

TRACK YOUR PROGRESS
- What Did You Learn?.. 194

Research and Inquiry... 195

 Digital Tools Find this eBook and other resources at **my.mheducation.com**

Chris Deeney/Alamy Stock Photo; (bkgd) Lissa Harrison

Talk About It

Essential Question

How do natural forces affect Earth?

Forces within our Earth often produce dramatic surface changes. Earth's crust is continually moving, causing volcanism and earthquakes. There are many active volcanoes in the United States. During certain types of eruptions, jets of molten rock called lava fountains reach temperatures of 2,000°F and spray as high as 1,600 feet into the air!

Look at the photograph. Talk to a partner about what you see. Discuss what occurs during a volcanic eruption. Fill in the chart with examples.

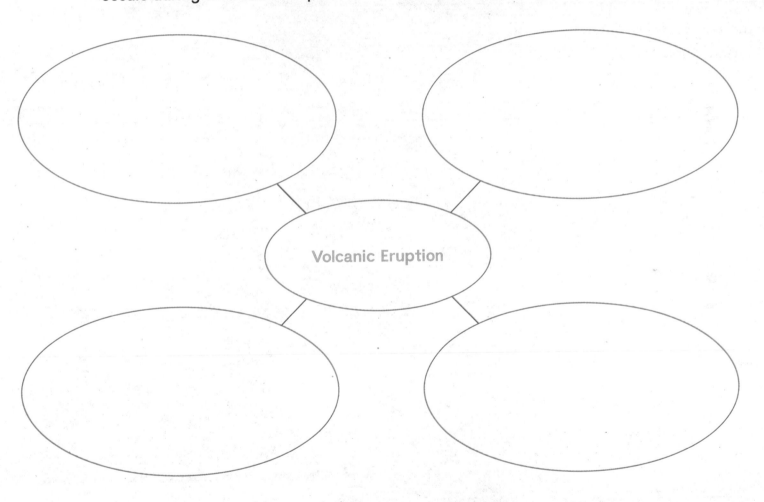

Volcanic Eruption

Go online to **my.mheducation.com** and read the "Nature's Sculptures" Blast. Think about what you know about how wind, moving water, and changing temperatures affect Earth's surface. How might brisk winds on a summer day or freezing temperatures change landscapes? Blast back your response.

TAKE NOTES

To help you focus as you read, preview the text and make a prediction about what you think will happen. Read the title and preview the text features. Then write your prediction below.

_____
_____
_____

As you read, take note of

Interesting Words _____

_____
_____
_____

Key Details _____

_____
_____
_____
_____

The Monster in the Mountain

Bettmann/Getty Images

Essential Question

How do natural forces affect Earth?

Read how a scientist studies forces that cause volcanic activity at Mount Vesuvius.

Meet Marta Ramírez

As a young girl during World War II, Marta Ramírez saw newsreels that showed B-25 airplanes flying near the smoky plume of a volcanic eruption. The year was 1944, and Mount Vesuvius in Italy was erupting! Blankets of burning ash were seen smothering the airplanes. **Shards** of volcanic rock came **plummeting** from the sky. Soldiers on the ground ran for cover. Each glowing splinter of rock was like a fiery dagger.

Those images never left Ramírez. She has been fascinated by volcanoes ever since. When she got older, Ramírez earned degrees in geology and volcanology. Though she has studied many of the world's volcanoes, she returns again and again to Mount Vesuvius. Ramírez has climbed down into its smoking crater many times. In the following memoir, she describes one of her visits and why this volcano still inspires her work.

At the Monster's Mouth

I recently went to see this **dynamic** volcano again. I decided to climb its slope along with the dozens of curious tourists visiting that day. As we walked, our shoes crunched on cinders that had been dropped there long ago. Finally reaching the rim, we gazed at the spectacular view. We stared 800 feet down into the crater. It was quiet for now, but I knew it was only sleeping. Frequent tremors and small earthquakes prove that this monster is not dead. Did the others standing there with me know about the danger beneath their feet?

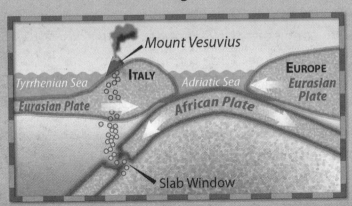

This model shows how Mount Vesuvius formed where one plate of Earth's crust pushes against another. Molten rock at this collision point exerts pressure upward until lava explodes from the volcano.

FIND TEXT EVIDENCE 🔍

Read

Paragraphs 1–2

Main Idea and Key Details

Underline key details in paragraphs 1 and 2. What is the central, or main, idea of the paragraphs?

_____

_____

_____

Paragraph 3

Reread

Draw a box around text evidence that tells why Mount Vesuvius could still be a danger one day.

Model

Circle the spot where two plates collided and caused Mount Vesuvius to form.

Reread

Author's Craft

Why did the author include the model showing the formation of Mount Vesuvius?

FIND TEXT EVIDENCE

Read

Paragraph 1
Metaphors and Similes

What does the author compare scalding lava to? **Underline** the text that shows this comparison. What does the author compare hard, dry lava to? **Circle** the text that shows this comparison.

Map

In what area of Italy is Mount Vesuvius located?

_____

_____

Paragraphs 2–3
Main Idea and Key Details

Look for key details in paragraph 3. **Draw a box** around the main idea.

Reread

Author's Craft

How does the author's language help you visualize an erupting volcano?

Every time I see this volcano up close, I think about how it had roared like a lion back in 1944. The trembling earth shook buildings for miles around, and streams of **scalding** lava flowed down the sides. Like glowing red fingers, they stretched out to crush defenseless homes below. It must have been terrifying to witness in person. Today, the lava that once **cascaded** down the mountain is hard and dry. It looks a bit like the skin of an elephant.

When the Monster Awakens

There is a lot of **documentation** of Vesuvius's past. Geologists have gathered this evidence of earlier eruptions by studying the rocks that were formed. Before 1944, the most catastrophic eruption occurred in 79 A.D. A Roman writer named Pliny the Younger described it in detail in his letters. On the morning of that tragic day, no one guessed that an enormous volcanic explosion was about to **pulverize** tons of rock and send it raining down on the city. People couldn't know that thick, dark ash and fiery lava would completely destroy the nearby cities of Pompeii and Herculaneum. By evening, few people had survived.

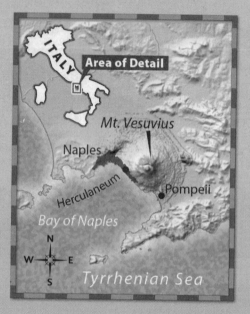

Many smaller eruptions have occurred since then, including the one in 1944. Volcanologists believe that another major eruption could occur at any time. The probability grows with each passing year. To watch for geological changes within Vesuvius, we have set up seismographs on the slopes of its cone. These instruments measure the slightest shifts in the rock beneath the mountain.

During one dangerous but exciting mission, I climbed down into the crater itself. My crew and I worked on mapping what was going on underground. We also measured the gases leaking from small vents. Any sudden increase in carbon dioxide and other gases might signal an eruption.

Looking Ahead

I don't go into the crater anymore, but I often think about how Vesuvius threatens the environment around it. Today, the city of Naples lies at the foot of Mount Vesuvius. If an eruption occurred tomorrow, the city would not be ready. Tons of ash and rock would once more be hurled into the air. This volcanic debris would keep cars, planes, and trains from operating. People would try escaping on foot. Sadly, no one can outrun such an eruption.

The only sure way to protect people who live near this volcano is to give them enough warning. The city of Naples has detailed evacuation plans. For the plans to work, however, officials need to be warned seven days before an eruption occurs. I hope the work that volcanologists do will help to give people the warning they need. Until then, I'll be watching this sleeping monster, just in case it starts to wake up.

Behind Vesuvius are the remains of Mount Somma, a volcano that erupted 25,000 years ago. Vesuvius formed inside Somma's crater.

Atlantide Phototravel/Corbis Documentary/Getty Images

Summarize

Use your notes to orally summarize Marta Ramírez's visit to Mount Vesuvius and why this volcano still inspires her work. Talk about whether your prediction from page 2 was confirmed or needed correction.

FIND TEXT EVIDENCE

Read

Paragraph 1

Reread

Draw a box around the text that explains why the crew measured the gases leaking from small vents.

Paragraphs 2–3

Metaphors and Similes

Underline the sentence which shows a comparison of two unlike things. What is being compared?

_____

_____

Make Inferences

Why does the author make the comparison noted above?

_____

_____

Reread

Author's Craft

Why do you think the author uses the subhead "Looking Ahead" for the last section of the text?

Vocabulary

Use the example sentences to talk with a partner about each word. Then answer the questions.

cascaded
As the sink overflowed, water **cascaded** onto the floor.

What else have you seen that cascaded?

_____

_____

documentation
Careful **documentation** of research is important when writing reports.

Why is documentation important?

_____

_____

dynamic
Because a tornado is so **dynamic**, it can quickly change course.

Why might dynamic weather events be dangerous?

_____

_____

exerts
Listening to soothing music **exerts** a positive effect on a person's mood.

What else exerts a positive effect on a person's mood?

_____

_____

plummeting
We watched the hail **plummeting** from the sky.

What else have you seen plummeting from up high?

_____

_____

Build Your Word List Pick a word you found interesting in the selection you read. Look up synonyms and antonyms of the word in a thesaurus and write them in your writer's notebook.

pulverize

We can **pulverize** coffee beans by grinding them.

What happens when you pulverize something?

_____

_____

scalding

You should let **scalding** soup cool before trying to eat it.

What might happen if you eat or drink something that is scalding?

_____

_____

shards

The flowerpot fell off the shelf and broke into many **shards**.

What else might break into shards if it falls?

_____

_____

Metaphors and Similes

A simile compares two unlike things or ideas using the words *like* or *as*. A metaphor compares two unlike things or ideas without using *like* or *as*. Comparisons help readers visualize events or ideas in a text.

 FIND TEXT EVIDENCE

I see the word like *in paragraph 1 on page 3:* Each glowing splinter of rock was like a fiery dagger. *This is a simile. In paragraph 3, I see Mount Vesuvius compared to a monster. This comparison does not use the words* like *or* as, *so it is a metaphor.*

Each glowing splinter of rock was like a fiery dagger.

Frequent tremors and small earthquakes prove that this monster is not dead.

Your Turn Reread the sentence below from page 4. Does the sentence contain a simile or a metaphor? What is being compared?

"Every time I see this volcano up close, I think about how it had roared like a lion back in 1944."

_____

_____

Bettmann/Getty Images

Reread

Rereading portions of "The Monster in the Mountain" can help you better understand facts about Mount Vesuvius and its volcanic eruptions.

🔍 FIND TEXT EVIDENCE

You may not be sure why volcanologists would study a volcano even when it isn't erupting. Reread "When the Monster Awakens" on page 4 of "The Monster in the Mountain."

Quick Tip

If you are unclear about information in a section of text, write down a question you have about the information. Then go back and reread the section, looking for the answer to your question.

Page 4

When the Monster Awakens

There is a lot of **documentation** of Vesuvius's past. Geologists have gathered this evidence of earlier eruptions by studying the rocks that were formed. Before 1944, the most catastrophic eruption occurred in 79 A.D. A Roman writer named Pliny the Younger described it in detail in his letters. On the morning of that tragic day, no one guessed that an enormous volcanic explosion was about to **pulverize** tons of rock and send it raining down on the city.

I read that scientists gather historical and geological documentation about the volcano's past. From this I can tell that learning about past eruptions helps predict when it may erupt again.

Your Turn How does information about past eruptions affect people living near Vesuvius today? Reread "Looking Ahead" on page 5. Remember to use the Reread strategy.

_____

_____

_____

_____

_____

_____

_____

Maps and Models

"The Monster in the Mountain" is mostly a first-person narrative written by a scientist. Narrative nonfiction gives factual information about a topic. It may tell one person's experiences or discuss events related to the topic. The author of a narrative nonfiction text describes events in a logical order.

FIND TEXT EVIDENCE

"The Monster in the Mountain" is a scientist's memoir written with the first-person pronouns I *and* we. *A map shows the location of Vesuvius. A model adds information about how Vesuvius formed.*

Readers to Writers

Writers use maps and models to illustrate information in a text. Study a model or a map, read its labels, and think about how it relates, or connects, to the topic. How does the model or map help you understand the text? What new information do you learn?

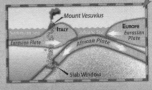

Page 3

Meet Marta Ramírez

As a young girl during World War II, Marta Ramírez saw newsreels that showed B-25 airplanes flying near the smoky plume of a volcanic eruption. The year was 1944, and Mount Vesuvius in Italy was erupting! Blankets of burning ash were seen smothering the airplanes. **Shards** of volcanic rock came **plummeting** from the sky. Soldiers on the ground ran for cover. Each glowing splinter of rock was like a fiery dagger.

Those images never left Ramírez. She has been fascinated by volcanoes ever since. When she got older, Ramírez earned degrees in geology and volcanology. Though she has studied many of the world's volcanoes, she returns again and again to Mount Vesuvius. Ramírez has climbed down into its smoking crater many times. In the following memoir, she describes one of her visits and why this volcano still inspires her work.

At the Monster's Mouth

I recently went to see this **dynamic** volcano again. I decided to climb its slope along with the dozens of curious tourists visiting that day. As we walked, our shoes crunched on cinders that had been dropped there long ago. Finally reaching the rim, we gazed at the spectacular view. We stared 800 feet down into the crater. It was quiet for now, but I knew it was only sleeping. Frequent tremors and small earthquakes prove that this monster is not dead. Did the others standing there with me know about the danger beneath their feet?

Mount Vesuvius — *ITALY* — *EUROPE* — *Eurasian Plate* — *African Plate* — *Eurasian Plate* — *Slab Window*

This model shows how Mount Vesuvius formed where one plate of Earth's crust pushes against another. Molten rock at this collision point exerts pressure upward until lava explodes from the volcano.

Maps

Maps show the locations of places discussed in the text.

Models

Models provide simple visual explanations of detailed factual information.

Your Turn Find two text features in "The Monster in the Mountain." Explain how each contributes to your understanding of the text.

_____

_____

_____

_____

_____

Main Idea and Key Details

The main idea is the most important point an author makes about a topic or in a section of text. The main idea may be stated or unstated. If it is not stated, readers can use key details to identify the main idea.

🔍 FIND TEXT EVIDENCE

When I reread "At the Monster's Mouth" on pages 3 and 4, I can ask myself what this section is mainly about. All of the key details together help me figure out the unstated main idea.

Main Idea
While Mount Vesuvius may currently be sleeping, the volcano could erupt again.
Detail
The 1944 eruption made the ground shake for miles around the volcano, and lava flowed down its sides.
Detail
Hardened lava from the 1944 eruption is still visible at the volcano.
Detail
Mount Vesuvius continues to show signs of activity.

Your Turn Reread "When the Monster Awakens" on pages 4–5. Find key details in the section and list them in the graphic organizer on page 11. Figure out what the details have in common to find the main idea of the section.

Main Idea
Detail
Detail
Detail

Respond to Reading

Discuss the prompt below. Think about how the author describes and presents the information. Use your notes and graphic organizer.

How does the author help you understand the ways in which Mount Vesuvius might affect people in the future?

_____

_____

_____

_____

_____

_____

_____

_____

_____

_____

_____

_____

Research Plan

A plan for collecting research from a variety of sources can help you stay focused and organized to finish a product. Consider what you already know about a topic and any key words and phrases related to it. Some features of a research plan are

- a list of print, video, audio, and digital sources;
- research questions, organized by topic;
- a method for taking notes and recording information.

What are some additional examples of print, digital, visual, and audio resources?

_____

_____

_____

Blog Report With a group, create a blog report about a natural disaster that has occurred in recent history. Decide as a group which disaster you will write your blog report about. Then consider these questions as you research and create the report:

- When and where did the disaster occur?
- What caused it?
- What effects did it have on people and the environment?

As a group, discuss how you will incorporate digital, audio, and video resources such as photos, hyperlinks, or audio clips into your report. After you finish, you will be sharing your blog report with your classmates.

Print resources:
newspapers, magazine articles

Digital resources:
encyclopedias, magazine articles

Visual resources:
photographs, videos

Audio resources:
interviews

The list above shows one student's plan for the types of sources she will use to collect information about a natural disaster.

 Tech Tip

Consider using an electronic note-taking tool to take notes as you research your topic.

Into the Volcano: A Volcano Researcher at Work

Literature Anthology:
pages 10–23

? **How does the author present information to help you understand more about volcanoes?**

COLLABORATE

Talk About It Reread **Literature Anthology** pages 12–13. Talk with a partner about the different features of this selection and how they help you better understand volcanoes.

Cite Text Evidence How does the author help you understand the topic better? Use the chart below to show three ways she does this and how it helps you.

How Volcanoes Form	Volcano Types	Models

Write The author helps me understand more about volcanoes by _____

_____

_____

Quick Tip

Sidebars give more information about a topic. Sometimes authors use color or a box to set off a sidebar from the main text. For example, on pages 12–13 the sidebars "How Volcanoes Form" and "Volcano Types" appear on a green background. Think about why an author might separate the main text from sidebars.

 Evaluate Information

Authors of nonfiction texts make choices about how they explain details about a topic. On page 12, why do you think the author uses models to give information?

Why is "A Walk on the Wild Side" a good heading for this section?

 Talk About It Reread **Literature Anthology** page 17. Talk with a partner about how the author describes the lava tubes.

Cite Text Evidence What details help you visualize the danger of being so close to a lava tube? Write text evidence here.

Detail

↓

Detail

↓

Detail

↓

How I Know

Write "A Walk on the Wild Side" is a good heading for this section

because _____

_____

_____

Sometimes an author uses a simile to help readers visualize what is happening. Notice when an author uses the words *like* and *as.* For example, on page 17 the word *like* signals the simile *like running over black crystal snowflakes made of glass.* When you read a simile, pause and think about the comparison the author is making. How can you use the comparison to visualize what the author is describing?

? **How do the author's real life experiences and descriptive language broaden your understanding of volcanoes?**

COLLABORATE

Talk About It Reread **Literature Anthology** page 19. Talk with a partner about how the author makes reading about volcanoes exciting.

Cite Text Evidence How does the author's descriptive language help you visualize what she experienced? Record text evidence in the chart.

Make Inferences

To gain a deeper understanding of the author's experience, infer how she felt as she tried to photograph the volcano. What effect might these emotions have on her description of the experience?

Text Evidence	Text Evidence	Text Evidence

Visualize

Write The author helps me understand more about volcanoes by _____

_____

_____

_____

Respond to Reading

COLLABORATE

Discuss the prompt below. Think about what you know about volcanoes and their effects. Use your notes and graphic organizer.

How does the author help you understand the effects of Kilauea on its surroundings and the people who live there?

_____

_____

_____

_____

_____

_____

_____

_____

_____

_____

_____

_____

_____

Donna O'Meara:
The Volcano Lady

Literature Anthology:
pages 26–29

1   After a blistering hot day, a cold storm suddenly whipped around the top of Mt. Stromboli, a volcano on an island off the coast of Sicily. The temperature quickly dropped over 60 degrees. Donna O'Meara and her husband, Steve, didn't dare try to climb down the steep slopes in the dark. They were stuck on a narrow ledge just 200 feet above a fiery, smoking pit. They huddled together, shivering nonstop in the cold air. Thundering blasts from the volcano and falling rocks the size of basketballs kept them awake and fearful. When the sun came up, Donna felt cinder burns on her face. There were sharp pieces of rock tangled in her hair.

2   Frightening experiences on top of a volcano are not unusual for Donna O'Meara. For over 25 years, she has worked with Steve to photograph and study volcanoes all over the world. They hope their documentation will someday be a written and visual record of information that helps scientists to better predict volcanic eruptions.

Reread paragraph 1. **Circle** words and phrases that the author uses to help you visualize what Donna O'Meara experienced at the top of Mt. Stromboli.

Now reread paragraph 2 and **underline** the sentence that transitions from what she experienced to what she does. Write it here:

_____

_____

_____

_____

COLLABORATE

Talk with a partner about why the author chose to include such a vivid description of what Donna O'Meara experienced.

Make marks in the margin next to the text evidence you used to support your discussion.

1　　From their home, Donna and Steve run Volcano Watch International (VWI). The O'Mearas' organization is dedicated to understanding how Earth's active volcanoes work. VWI uses photos and video to educate people about the dangers of volcanoes. Their mission is to travel to active volcanoes and document the eruptions.

2　　The first volcano Donna studied was Kilauea, which is a shield volcano. Mt. Stromboli is a stratovolcano. A stratovolcano has the common cone shape people usually picture when they think of a volcano. It is formed from explosive eruptions that build layers of ash, lava, and cinders at the top of the mountain.

3　　Donna says the experience of being stranded on Mt. Stromboli for one freezing night was the scariest experience of her life. Since the sides of this volcano are steep, it was impossible for the O'Mearas to travel down the slopes until the sun rose in the morning. So they were trapped on the ledge in the freezing cold with scalding rocks flying around them.

Reread paragraph 1. **Underline** Volcano Watch International's mission. **Circle** clues in the paragraph that describe what they do.

Place a star at the end of the sentence in paragraph 2 that helps you understand more about Mt. Stromboli.

COLLABORATE

Reread paragraph 3. Talk about why knowing the shape of a stratovolcano adds to your understanding of Donna O'Meara's scary night on top of Mt. Stromboli.

Draw a box around one more clue that describes a stratovolcano. Write it here:

_____

_____

_____

_____

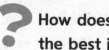

? **How does the author show that Donna O'Meara believes she has the best job on Earth?**

COLLABORATE

Talk About It Reread the excerpts on pages 18 and 19. Talk with a partner about clues that help you figure out why the O'Mearas love what they do.

Cite Text Evidence What words and phrases does the author use to show that the O'Mearas love their job? Write text evidence below.

Quick Tip

When you cite text evidence, you use the words or phrases from a selection you read in your response. The text evidence should support your answer.

Clues	
	Donna and Steve O'Meara love their job.

Write I know Donna O'Meara loves her job because _____

_____

_____

_____

_____

Print and Graphic Features

Authors include different **print** and **graphic** features to help readers understand a topic. Some features include headings, maps, and models. Photographs and captions also support a writer's ideas.

🔍 FIND TEXT EVIDENCE

Look at the photograph from **Literature Anthology** page 28, at the bottom right, and read the caption. The author includes these features to provide evidence that some people live extremely close to a volcano.

Your Turn Look at the model on **Literature Anthology** page 29 and think about the photograph and caption on page 28.

- What is the purpose of the model? _____

  _____

  _____

  _____

- How does the model help you understand what will happen to the village pictured on page 28 when Mt. Stromboli erupts again? _____

  _____

  _____

  _____

  _____

Readers to Writers

Other print and graphic features you can add to your writing include timelines, charts, and graphs. These features help you explain your ideas in a more visual, interesting way.

A village is quite close to the volcano on the island of Stromboli. Millions of people around the world live near active volcanoes.

Marco Simoni/Cultura Creative (RF)/Alamy Stock Photo

Text Connections

? How is the way the artist uses color and technique to paint the ocean similar to the way Donna O'Meara uses words and phrases to describe volcanoes in the selections you read this week?

Talk About It With a partner, talk about what you see in the painting. Discuss how the painting makes you feel.

Cite Text Evidence How does the feeling you get from looking at this painting compare to Donna's description of being stuck on top of Mt. Stromboli? **Circle** clues in the painting that help you make that comparison.

Write Like O'Meara's description of

volcanoes, Thomas Chambers _____

_____

_____

_____

_____

_____

_____

_____

American artist Thomas Chambers painted *Storm-Tossed Frigate* in the mid-nineteenth century. An oil painting on canvas, it is now owned by the National Gallery of Art in Washington, D.C.

Present Your Work

Discuss how you will present your blog report about a natural disaster, including how you will present any print, digital, audio, and video resources. Discuss the sentence starters below and write your answers.

Use the Listening Checklist as your classmates give their presentation.

After learning more about a natural disaster that occurred

in recent history, I _____

_____

_____

I am interested in finding out more about _____

_____

_____

Iakov Filimonov/Shutterstock

*Literature Anthology:
pages 10–23*

Expert Model

Features of a Personal Narrative

A personal narrative is a piece of nonfiction writing that tells a story from the author's life. A personal narrative

- is usually told from the first-person point of view and expresses the writer's thoughts and feelings about an experience;

- follows a logical sequence of events;

- uses vivid descriptions to help readers imagine the experience.

Analyze an Expert Model Studying a personal narrative will help you write one of your own. Reread page 22 of *Into the Volcano* in the **Literature Anthology** and answer the questions below.

What details from the text tell you that this section of *Into the Volcano* is a

personal narrative? _____

_____

Look at the paragraphs on page 22. List four examples of phrases the

author uses to show a sequence of events.

1 _____

2 _____

3 _____

4 _____

> ### Word Wise
>
> In the caption on page 22, notice the phrases *rare moment* and *lucky enough*. These phrases focus the reader on understanding how the author feels about what she is experiencing.

Plan: Choose Your Topic

Freewrite Think about experiences that have had a strong impact on you, such as starting at a new school, going on a special trip, participating in a community service project, or adopting a new pet. Quickly write your ideas below without stopping. Then discuss your ideas with a partner.

_____

_____

_____

Writing Prompt Choose one important experience that had an impact on you from your freewriting. Then write a personal narrative about it.

I will write my personal narrative about _____

Purpose and Audience Think about who will read or hear your narrative. Will your purpose be to inform, persuade, or entertain? Think about the language you will use to write your narrative.

My purpose is to _____

My audience will be _____

I will use _____ language when I write my personal narrative.

Plan Think about what you want your readers to learn about the experience. Ask yourself questions and answer them in your writer's notebook. Questions might include: _Why was the experience important to me? What did I learn from it? How do I feel about what happened?_ Include specific details in your answers.

Plan: Sequence

Sequence of Events After choosing a topic, you will need to plan how to use a logical sequence of events to tell your personal narrative. The order in which you describe the events that make up your experience will help readers better understand why the events impacted you. Ask yourself:

- Am I telling the events in an order that is logical and easy to follow?

- Am I leaving out details about an important event? Am I including details about an event that is not important?

- Do I use transition words and phrases such as *yesterday, later in the afternoon,* or *meanwhile* to show a chronological sequence of events that takes readers from the beginning of the experience to the end?

List three events you will tell about in the sequence of your narrative.

1 _____

_____

2 _____

_____

3 _____

_____

 Graphic Organizer In your writer's notebook, create a Sequence of Events map to plan your writing. Fill in the boxes with the main events of your personal narrative in order. Include only the most important details.

Quick Tip

Transition words and phrases connect ideas and help readers better understand a narrative's timeline. Not all transition words are related to time, though. Some can signal contrast, addition, and logical relationships. Consider adding words such as *however, although, nevertheless, similarly, moreover,* and other signal words where they make sense.

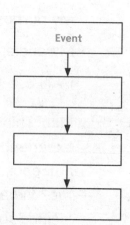

Event

Draft

Develop Experiences Writers include details and vivid, descriptive language to explain how an event changed the way they think or how they felt about the experience. In this excerpt from "The Monster in the Mountain," the author expresses a sense of dread about the volcano.

> It was quiet for now, but I knew it was only sleeping. Frequent tremors and small earthquakes prove that this monster is not dead. Did the others standing there with me know about the danger beneath their feet?

Word Wise

Personification is a type of figurative language that gives human qualities to nonhuman things. Do you think it was appropriate for the author of this personal narrative to use personification?

Now use the excerpt as a model to write a paragraph that could be part of your personal narrative. Think carefully about your descriptions.

_____

_____

_____

_____

Write a Draft Use your Sequence of Events map to write your draft in your writer's notebook. Include transitions to show the order of events and vivid descriptions to help readers understand the impact of your experience.

Digital Tools

For more information on how to plan events in your personal narrative, watch "Story Map to Draft." Go to **my.mheducation.com.**

Revise

Word Choice Authors of personal narratives choose their words carefully to help readers understand their emotions. They include precise verbs, vivid adjectives, and figurative language to express feelings and establish mood. Read the paragraph below. Then revise the first three sentences by replacing everyday language with more precise, descriptive language to emphasize strong feelings or mood. Expand on the experience by adding important and interesting details.

> After picking up trash, I felt sad. There was so much garbage in the park. I asked our group leader, Mr. Wong, "Why do people leave trash where kids play?" He shook his head and said, "It's terrible, but I take out my frustration on the trash. Like this!" Then he showed me what he meant by using his stick to pick up a soda cup from the ground.

 Revision Revise your draft and check that you used words that help your reader understand how you are feeling. Make sure it shows why the experience had an impact on you.

Grammar Connections

As you revise, make sure your dialogue is correctly punctuated. Lines of dialogue should be set off by quotation marks. Use a comma to separate a phrase, such as *I said*, from the quotation itself. Place the end punctuation inside the quotation marks when it is part of the quote. For example, *Mr. Wong shook his head and said, "It's terrible."*

Peer Conferences

Review a Draft Listen carefully as a partner reads his or her work aloud. Take notes about what you liked and what was difficult to follow. Begin by telling what you liked about the draft. Ask questions that will help the writer think more about the writing. Make suggestions that you think will make the writing stronger. Use these sentence starters.

I enjoyed this part of your draft because . . .

You might improve this description by . . .

I have a question about . . .

I am not sure about the order of . . .

Partner Feedback After your partner gives you feedback on your draft, write one of the suggestions that you will use in your revision. Refer to the rubric on page 31 as you give feedback.

Based on my partner's feedback, I will _____

_____

_____

_____

After you finish giving each other feedback, reflect on the peer conference. What was helpful? What might you do differently next time?

Revision As you revise your draft, use the Revising Checklist to help you figure out what text you may need to move, elaborate on, or delete. Remember to use the rubric on page 31 to help you with your revision.

Revising Checklist

- [ ] Does my writing fit my purpose and audience?
- [ ] Do I use transition words and phrases to make my sequence of events clear and logical?
- [ ] Do I use words that are descriptive and precise?
- [ ] Do I clearly express my feelings and thoughts about the experience in order to establish mood?

Edit and Proofread

Tech Tip

Use your spelling checker thoughtfully by highlighting and spell-checking your personal narrative paragraph by paragraph. Reviewing your writing in sections will help you focus better on each error the spelling checker finds. Make sure you understand the error and agree with the correction before you accept any changes.

When you **edit** and **proofread** your writing, you look for and correct mistakes in spelling, punctuation, capitalization, and grammar. Reading through a revised draft multiple times can help you make sure you're correcting any errors. Use the checklist below to edit your sentences.

✔ Editing Checklist

☐ Are quotation marks used correctly?

☐ Do all sentences begin with a capital letter and end with a punctuation mark?

☐ Do all sentences express a complete thought?

☐ Are there any run-on sentences or fragments to correct?

☐ Are commas used correctly?

☐ Are all words spelled correctly?

List two mistakes you found as you proofread your personal narrative.

1 _____

_____

_____

2 _____

_____

_____

Publish, Present, and Evaluate

Publishing When you **publish** your writing, you create a clean, neat final copy that is free of mistakes. If you are writing in cursive, be sure to write legibly and to leave spaces between words.

Presentation When you are ready to **present** your work, rehearse your presentation. Use the Presenting Checklist to help you.

Evaluate After you publish your writing, use the rubric below to **evaluate** your writing.

What did you do successfully? _____

What needs more work? _____

_____

4	3	2	1
• uses plenty of precise language to tell about a personal experience, including why the experience was impactful • has a logical sequence of events with transition words to connect events • includes plenty of descriptive language and figurative language to create a mood and help readers understand the experience	• uses some precise language to tell about a personal experience, including why the experience was impactful • has a mostly logical sequence of events with some transition words to connect events • includes some descriptive language and figurative language to create a mood and help readers understand the experience	• tells about a personal experience but does not explain why it was impactful • lacks a logical sequence of events with few transition words to connect events • includes little descriptive language to create a mood and help readers understand the experience	• does not share a personal experience • does not have a logical sequence of events • does not include descriptive language to create a mood and help readers understand the experience

Talk About It

Essential Question

How do new experiences offer new perspectives?

The people in the photograph live in a big city. It can be hard to see stars at night in a city because the city lights can make the sky too bright for even a glimmer of stars to show. In the country, it is possible to have another perspective of the night sky.

Look at the photograph and discuss with a partner what new perspectives the people might be gaining. Then describe an experience you had that gave you a new perspective. Fill in the web with ways in which new experiences can offer new perspectives.

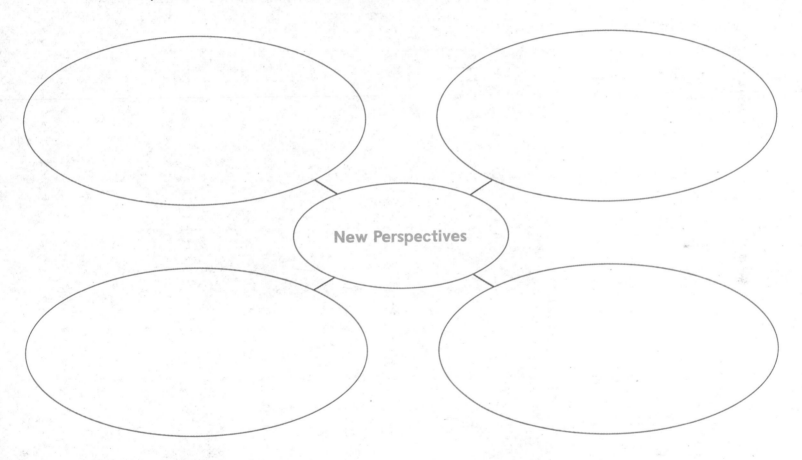

New Perspectives

Go online to **my.mheducation.com** and read the "From Months to Seconds" Blast. Think about how innovations in technology offer people a new perspective on communication. What could change our view of communication in the future? Blast back your response.

TAKE NOTES

Making predictions helps you focus your reading. Use the illustrations and what you know about realistic fiction stories to make a prediction. As you read, you can see if your prediction is confirmed or if you need to correct it. This will help you check your understanding. Write your prediction below.

_____

_____

_____

As you read, take note of

Interesting Words _____

_____

_____

_____

Key Details _____

_____

_____

_____

_____

COW Music

Essential Question

? How do new experiences offer new perspectives?

Read about the way a girl's outlook changes when she moves to a new home.

Farewell to Me

I crammed one last box into the back seat and slammed the car door. It felt as if I were slamming the door on my whole life. At first, I was thrilled when Mom told me she'd gotten a fantastic new job as a veterinarian at an animal hospital. Then, because she always saves the bad news for last, she told me the really **heinous** part. The hospital wasn't in our city; it was miles away in the middle of nowhere. And I'm definitely *not* a country girl.

I slouched against the car, taking a last look at our building. To most people, it probably just looks like any other old apartment house, but I love every grimy brick. Soon I'd be staring at piles of hay.

Just then, I heard a bright blast of music and saw my best friends, Hana and Leo, come charging up to me. While Hana played a cool riff on her trumpet, Leo sang, "We will miss you, Celia . . . At least you won't be in Australia." I raised my eyebrows.

Greg Newbold

Laughing, Leo said, "Hey, *you* find something to rhyme with *Celia!*"

"You guys are utterly **indispensable!**" I blurted out. "How will I live without you?"

"Ever hear of texting?" asked Hana, punctuating her question with a loud trumpet honk. I jumped into the car fast so no one could see me tear up. As Mom pulled away, I waved goodbye to my friends, my neighborhood, and my life.

We rode a while in silence, and I wedged my violin case beneath my legs for comfort. Leo, Hana, and I had been writing songs for our band, but that was all over now. "Don't think of this as an ending," Mom said, with her knack for reading my mind. "It's an exciting beginning, and we're on the **threshold** of a breathtaking new adventure."

"Yeah, it'll be great. I couldn't be happier," I said glumly.

"Don't be **sarcastic**, *mija*," Mom said. "It's so unattractive."

FIND TEXT EVIDENCE

Read

Paragraphs 1–6

Character, Setting, Plot

Circle the name of the main character of the story. **Underline** the problem the main character has. Why is the main character upset?

_____

_____

Paragraphs 7–9

Visualize

Draw a box around the sentence that describes the car ride.

Make Inferences

Why do you think Celia and Mom are quiet at the start of the car ride?

_____

_____

Reread

Author's Craft

Why is "Farewell to Me" a good title for this section?

SHARED READ

FIND TEXT EVIDENCE

Read

Paragraphs 1–5

Character, Setting, Plot

Circle words that tell you how Celia feels about the city. **Underline** words that tell you how she feels about the country.

Paragraphs 6–8

Narrator and Dialogue

Whose thoughts and feelings do you learn about in this part of the text?

_____

_____

Draw a box around the dialogue. Why does Celia say what she says?

_____

_____

_____

_____

Reread

Author's Craft

How does first-person point of view affect the mood of the story?

Being attractive wasn't a big goal at the moment, but annoying Mom wasn't either. So I clammed up and looked out the window as crowded, exciting city streets turned first into bland suburban shopping strips and then into endless, boring trees and fields of corn.

"Look: cows!" Mom said, as we cruised past some black-and-white blotches in a pasture.

"Sure, they seem sweet," I said, "but I bet they have a mean streak when you're not looking."

"It's normal to be a bit **phobic** about unfamiliar things," Mom said, in her best patient-parent tone. "But you don't need to be afraid of cows. They're harmless."

"Harmless . . . and boring," I thought to myself. "Like everything in the country."

Not So Bad?

We finally arrived at our new home, a two-story wooden farmhouse. It had a crooked roof, a rickety front porch, and too many places for bats to hide. "Would you mind if I don't go in yet?" I asked.

Mom looked overwhelmed. She just nodded and said I could go explore. I felt a **glimmer** of hope, a small hint that country life might turn out okay. Mom never let me go out alone in the city, so maybe a bit more freedom would be one **consolation** of living here.

I wandered off, clutching my violin and not paying attention to where I was going. It didn't matter; it was all just a blur of green and brown. I imagined that a big Saturday night here meant sitting around talking about corn . . . or watching it grow.

Suddenly I heard something I wasn't expecting—a blaring, jazzy tune. I pushed through some corn only to come face-to-face with an enormous cow. Then another hot jazz riff floated through the air. I spun around and saw a tall kid playing a beat-up old saxophone in the clearing. His music was fantastic, and he didn't dress the way I figured a country kid would. Where were the muddy dungarees and plaid bandana? This guy was wearing clothes that made him look cool, like a famous performer.

Not Bad at All!

I couldn't resist, so I took out my violin and began to play along. The boy looked surprised, but he didn't miss a beat. We improvised a cool duet, and by the end—no kidding—the big cow's tail was swishing to the rhythm. "I'm Jason," he said when we finished. "I play out here because the cows don't complain when I mess up. You must be Celia. My dad said you were moving in. I can't believe you play violin! I've been looking for someone to write songs with."

I looked at Jason and his dented sax, the cheerful cow and tall corn, the majestic trees in the distance, and the sun shining in the brilliant blue sky. I could feel my **perception** of country life already changing, and I had a feeling it would change a lot more.

FIND TEXT EVIDENCE

Read

Paragraphs 1–2

Context Clues

Underline words that help you determine the meaning of *duet*. Define *duet*.

_____

_____

Paragraph 3

Character, Setting, Plot

How does meeting Jason change Celia's feelings about the country?

_____

_____

_____

Visualize

Draw a box around the words that tell how Celia views the country now.

Reread

Author's Craft

What message does the author give readers through Celia's actions?

Summarize

Use your notes to orally summarize the story. Be sure to include details about the key events in the story and how the main character changes. Talk about whether your prediction from page 34 was confirmed or if it needed correction.

Vocabulary

Use the example sentences to talk with a partner about each word. Then answer the questions.

consolation

One **consolation** of losing was knowing he had done his best.

How do you provide consolation to a friend?

_____

_____

glimmer

My dog shows a **glimmer** of excitement when it is time to play.

What makes you feel a glimmer of excitement?

_____

_____

heinous

The children's **heinous** table manners made it unpleasant to eat with them.

What is an example of heinous table manners?

_____

_____

indispensable

A ball and bat are **indispensable** to playing baseball.

What items do you find indispensable during the school day?

_____

_____

perception

Our **perception** that our grandmother was happy made us smile.

What might cause you to have the perception that a friend is sad?

_____

_____

 Build Your Word List Reread the first paragraph on page 37. Mark the word *performer*. In your writer's notebook, use a word web to write more forms of the word. For example, write *perform*. Use a dictionary to help you find more related words.

phobic

Many people are **phobic** about going to the dentist.

Describe something you are phobic about.

_____

_____

_____

sarcastic

Her **sarcastic** comment hurt her friend's feelings.

Why are sarcastic comments often hurtful?

_____

_____

_____

threshold

The invention of the compass was the **threshold** for a new age of navigation.

What other innovations could be considered a threshold for something new?

_____

_____

_____

Context Clues

When you read an unfamiliar or multiple-meaning word, carefully reread the sentence in which it appears. Look for context clues in the sentence to help you figure out the word's meaning.

FIND TEXT EVIDENCE

I'm not sure what the word knack _means on page 35 of "Cow Music." I see that the phrase_ for reading my mind _comes after it in the sentence. "Reading" someone's mind is not easy to do, so this tells me that a_ knack _must be a skill for doing something well._

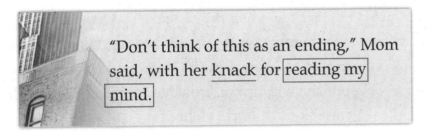

"Don't think of this as an ending," Mom said, with her knack for reading my mind.

Your Turn Use context clues to figure out the meanings of the following words in "Cow Music."

rickety, _page 36_ _____

_____

majestic, _page 37_ _____

_____

Visualize

To visualize something is to form a mental picture of it. Use the descriptions of settings, characters, and events in a story to imagine what they look like. As you read on, use details from the text to add to or change your mental images.

🔍 FIND TEXT EVIDENCE

You may not be sure why Celia is unhappy about moving to the country. Reread the first paragraph on page 36. Look for details that help you visualize the differences Celia sees between her old neighborhood and her new one.

Page 36

> Being attractive wasn't a big goal at the moment, but annoying Mom wasn't either. So I clammed up and looked out the window as crowded, exciting city streets turned first into bland suburban shopping strips and then into endless, boring trees and fields of corn.

I read that Celia could see "crowded, exciting city streets" change to "endless, boring trees and fields of corn." I can infer that Celia thinks the country will be much less interesting than the city.

Your Turn Reread the first paragraph on page 37. Why is this event important to the story? As you read, remember to use the strategy Visualize. Look for details that help you form a mental picture of the scene.

_____

_____

_____

_____

Narrator and Dialogue

"Cow Music" is realistic fiction. Characters in realistic fiction look and act like real people. They often engage in dialogue, or conversation. The settings are places that could be real. The narrator may be a character.

🔍 FIND TEXT EVIDENCE

As I started reading "Cow Music," I wondered who "I" was. As I read on, I understood that the character Celia is telling the story. She is the narrator. I also learn about the characters from their dialogue.

Page 35

Farewell to Me

I crammed one last box into the back seat and slammed the car door. It felt as if I were slamming the door on my whole life. At first, I was thrilled when Mom told me she'd gotten a fantastic new job as a veterinarian at an animal hospital. Then, because she always saves the bad news for last, she told me the really **heinous** part. The hospital wasn't in our city; it was miles away in the middle of nowhere. And I'm definitely *not* a country girl.

I slouched against the car, taking a last look at our building. To most people, it probably just looks like any other old apartment house, but I love every grimy brick. Soon I'd be staring at piles of hay.

Just then, I heard a bright blast of music and saw my best friends, Hana and Leo, come charging up to me. While Hana played a cool riff on her trumpet, Leo sang, "We will miss you, Celia . . . At least you won't be in Australia." I raised my eyebrows.

Laughing, Leo said, "Hey, *you* find something to rhyme with *Celia!*"

"You guys are utterly **indispensable!**" I blurted out: "How will I live without you?"

"Ever hear of texting?" asked Hana, punctuating her question with a loud trumpet honk. I jumped into the car fast so no one could see me tear up. As Mom pulled away, I waved goodbye to my friends, my neighborhood, and my life.

We rode a while in silence and I wedged my violin case beneath my legs for comfort. Leo, Hana, and I had been writing songs for our band, but that was all over now. "Don't think of this as an ending," Mom said with her knack for reading my mind. "It's an exciting beginning, and we're on the **threshold** of a breathtaking new adventure."

"Yeah, it'll be great. I couldn't be happier," I said glumly.

"Don't be **sarcastic**, *mija*," Mom said. "It's so unattractive."

Narrator

The narrator is the "voice" that tells the story.

Dialogue

Dialogue is what the characters say. Their exact words are placed inside quotation marks.

Your Turn Tell how the story would be different if Celia's mother were the narrator.

COLLABORATE

_____

_____

_____

Read aloud a line of dialogue in "Cow Music." What does it tell you about the character?

_____

_____

_____

Readers to Writers

Dialogue often reveals the thoughts and feelings of a character. It can also help you understand how a character solves a problem or what a character learns. Think about how you can use dialogue in your own writing.

Character, Setting, Plot

In fiction, changes to the **setting** often affect **characters** and shape events in the **plot**. As you read stories, such as "Cow Music," comparing and contrasting details from different settings can help you make inferences about the ways characters act. It can also help you understand the most important plot events.

FIND TEXT EVIDENCE

As I reread the first section of "Cow Music," I see that Celia thinks leaving the city means waving "goodbye to . . . my life." Though her mother calls the move "a breathtaking new adventure," Celia feels during the car ride that everything in the country will be "boring."

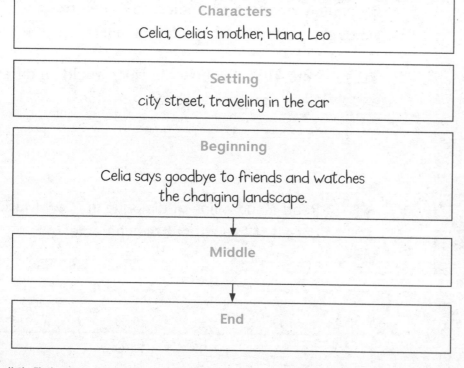

Characters
Celia, Celia's mother, Hana, Leo

Setting
city street, traveling in the car

Beginning
Celia says goodbye to friends and watches the changing landscape.

↓

Middle

↓

End

Your Turn Reread the rest of "Cow Music." Identify additional characters, settings, and key plot events to add to the graphic organizer on page 43. Include how Celia feels about her new home.

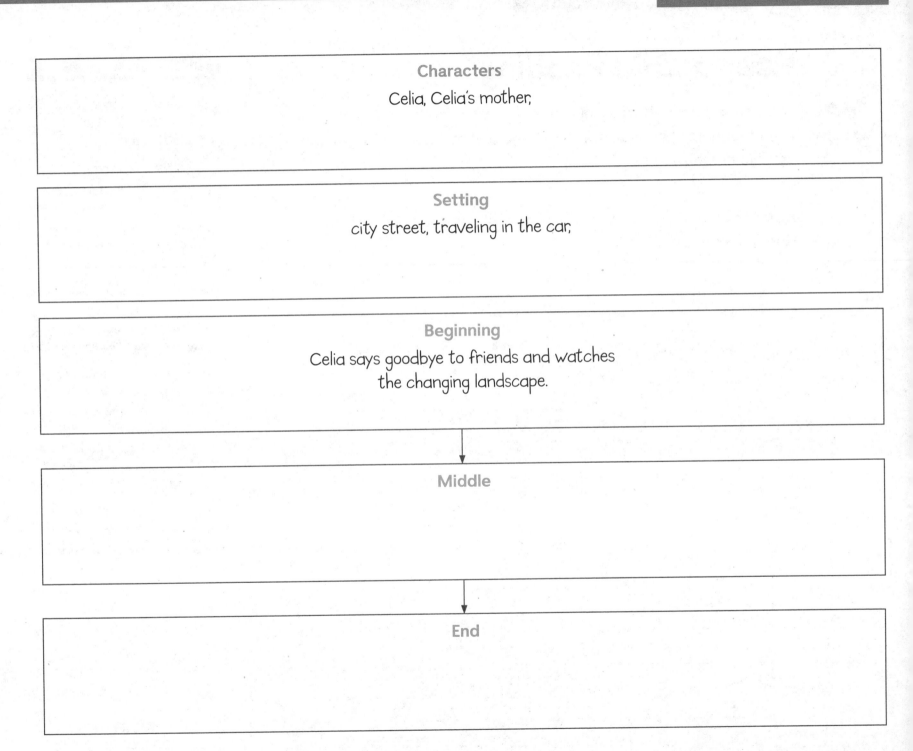

Characters

Celia, Celia's mother,

Setting

city street, traveling in the car,

Beginning

Celia says goodbye to friends and watches
the changing landscape.

Middle

End

Respond to Reading

Discuss the prompt below. Think about how the author lets you know what the main character is thinking and feeling. Use your notes and graphic organizer.

How does the author show how Celia's feelings about living in the country change?

_____

_____

_____

_____

_____

_____

_____

_____

_____

_____

_____

_____

Relevant Information

Relevant information is directly connected to the topic you are researching. As you research, you'll likely find information that, while interesting, does not provide the best support for the specific ideas you want to cover. To gather useful and relevant information

- focus your topic by writing a question that clarifies the purpose of your research;
- list and use search terms that directly reflect your purpose;
- use multiple print and digital sources.

What is something else you can do to gather relevant information?

_____

_____

The telephone provided the telegraph industry with more competition by creating a new form of communication.

COLLABORATE

Create an Advertisement In *Little Blog on the Prairie*, you will read about a family that stays at a camp that lacks modern inventions, such as indoor plumbing and refrigeration. With a partner or in a group, research a 19th century invention that people found useful. Then create an advertisement for the invention. Consider these questions:

- What was the invention? Who invented it and when?
- What did the invention do? What did people do before it was invented?
- How did the invention affect the people of the time period?

Discuss what print and digital sources you might use to gather relevant information. Be sure to add illustrations or photos to your advertisement. You will be sharing your advertisement with your classmates.

Little Blog on the Prairie

Literature Anthology:
pages 30–43

? How does the author use dialogue to help you understand how the characters feel?

COLLABORATE

Talk About It Reread the dialogue on **Literature Anthology** page 35. Talk about how Gen's family deals with life at the camp.

Cite Text Evidence What words and phrases tell you how the characters feel? Cite and explain text evidence.

Dialogue	What Happens	How Characters Feel
"You want it raw?" "I'm hungry."	Gavin asks to eat grits raw because he is so hungry.	Gavin feels hungry and impatient.

Write The author uses dialogue to _____

_____

_____

Quick Tip

Use your own experience to help you understand how the dialogue conveys the way the characters are feeling. Think about how you might react to being in a new situation. What would you say, and how might your words reveal how you feel?

Make Inferences

Characters don't always state exactly how they feel about a situation. It's up to readers to "read between the lines" and infer how the character feels. For example, Gavin doesn't say outright that he's impatient. How does the dialogue between Gavin and his mom help you infer that?

? **How does the author create tension between Nora and Gen?**

COLLABORATE

Talk About It Reread **Literature Anthology** pages 36–37. Talk with a partner about what you notice about how Nora and Gen interact.

Cite Text Evidence What clues help you know how Nora feels about Gen? Find evidence and explain how it creates tension.

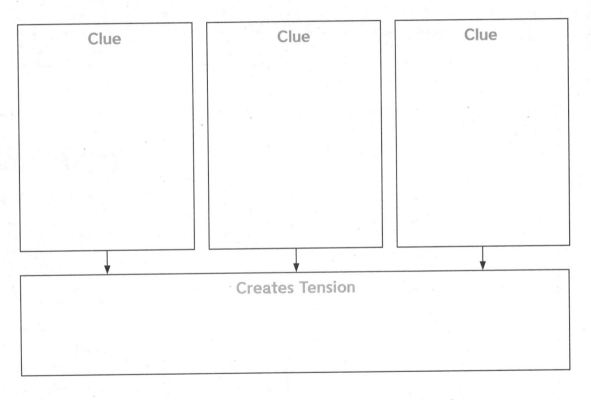

Clue	Clue	Clue

Creates Tension

Write The author creates tension between Nora and Gen by _____

_____

_____

_____

? How does the author use Gen's text messages to help you understand how she is dealing with her new experience?

COLLABORATE

Talk About It Reread the text messages on **Literature Anthology** page 40 and the first paragraph of page 41. Talk with a partner about why the text messages are important to the story.

Cite Text Evidence What words and phrases in Gen's text messages tell you about how she feels? Record evidence in the chart.

Text Evidence	How It Helps

Write The author uses Gen's text messages to show _____

_____

_____

_____

Respond to Reading

COLLABORATE Discuss the prompt below. Apply your knowledge of how dialogue and point of view can reveal a character's thinking to inform your answer. Use your notes and graphic organizer.

How does the author help you understand how new experiences can change the way we think?

_____

_____

_____

_____

_____

_____

_____

_____

_____

_____

_____

Eureka/Alamy Stock Photo

The Writing on the Wall

Literature Anthology:
pages 46–49

1   The small town of Allen Crossing, Indiana, has been the place I've called home for all 14 years of my life. That's where I spend hours just looking. Looking at how the wind makes the wild flowers of a meadow weave and sway to create a magical moving carpet of color. Looking at the way insects dart and dash among plants and blossoms in displays of frantic activity.

2   The beauty and drama of nature have always been what drives me to create art. I used to think that all true artists get inspiration from nature. Then I went to New York City and something happened that really made me rethink that idea.

3   I applied to an art college in New York that was offering two-week courses to middle school students with portfolios that showed they were serious about art. To be honest, I applied mostly because I liked the idea of putting my portfolio up against the work of other young artists. I wanted to see if I could get in.

Reread paragraph 1. **Underline** words and phrases that show how the narrator feels about Allen Crossing.

Reread paragraph 2. **Circle** how you know what the narrator thinks about inspiration.

COLLABORATE

Talk with a partner about where the narrator has always found inspiration. How do you know that his opinion will change later in the story?

Make a mark in the margin beside the sentences that signal change. Write them here:

_____

_____

_____

_____

_____

1. "It's a legal graffiti exhibit space." Myles said, "like a big gallery for street art." He explained that he and LeShawn and Pete had been selected to paint there in a contest their school had held before summer recess. They showed me sketches of what they planned to paint, and then I turned my gaze to the factory again. What I saw was art not unlike what I had been making. The big difference was, along with images from nature, the artists also drew images from city life. There was a subway train crammed with people rushing off to work and there were tall, shiny buildings stretching up into the sky. In every sketch, there was an energy that reminded me of that first subway ride, only it was a creative energy, not a panicky energy.

2. What I learned that summer in New York was indispensable to me, for now I know that inspiration is different for everyone. What drives one person crazy can be the thing that drives another to create. I may not look at the city the way Myles, LeShawn, and Pete do, but they may not see nature the way I do. I respect the way the city's energy inspires them.

Reread paragraph 1. **Underline** clues that show the narrator is changing his point of view about art.

Place a star beside the sentence that expresses his new perspective.

COLLABORATE

Reread paragraph 2. **Circle** text that shows how the narrator feels about inspiration. Talk about the two lessons he has learned. Number the sentences that reveal those lessons. Write the sentences here:

1. _____

_____

_____

_____

_____

2. _____

_____

_____

_____

How does the author show a change in the narrator from the beginning to the end of the selection?

Talk About It Reread the excerpts on pages 50–51. With a partner, discuss how the narrator feels about inspiration.

Cite Text Evidence Compare and contrast the narrator's feelings from the beginning to the end of the selection. Write text evidence in the chart.

Beginning	End

Write The author shows how the narrator changes by _____

_____

_____

_____

FabrikaSimf/Shutterstock

Imagery

Writers use imagery when they describe ideas, actions, people, or things with words and phrases that create mental images in a reader's mind. These words and phrases often appeal to a reader's senses, making it easier for the reader to visualize the scene. Imagery can also affect mood, or the feeling the writing creates.

FIND TEXT EVIDENCE

In "The Writing on the Wall" on **Literature Anthology** page 46, the imagery in the first paragraph helps the author convey the wind's effect on the flowers. The vivid verbs *weave* and *sway* help readers visualize the flowers moving gently back and forth in the wind and better understand why the author calls the scene a "magical moving carpet of color."

> Looking at how the wind makes the wild flowers of a meadow weave and sway to create a magical moving carpet of color.

Your Turn Reread the rest of pages 46 and 47.

- How does the author use imagery to help you visualize the city?

  _____

  _____

- How does the author's use of imagery show the contrast between the city and the country? _____

  _____

To add imagery to your own writing, think about what you want your readers to see, hear, feel, smell, or taste. Choose words that evoke these images. Also think about the mood of your writing. If you want a sad, excited, happy, or anxious mood, choose imagery that helps to set and maintain that mood.

Text Connections

? **How is the sculptor in the photograph using art to share a perspective in the same way that the characters do in *Little Blog on the Prairie* and "The Writing on the Wall"?**

Talk About It Talk about the photograph and caption. Discuss how the girl is using art to express a new perspective.

Cite Text Evidence How does creating art show others how you feel? **Circle** clues in the photograph and caption that indicate how art can be a medium for sharing feelings and perspectives.

Write The sculptor and characters I read about this week use their art _____

_____

_____

_____

_____

_____

_____

This middle school student is using a water-based clay to create a sculpture. The assignment was to think of someone she admires and create a piece of art that represents how she feels.

Writers and sculptors express a perspective through their art. Compare the sculptor's work with Gen's writing and the work of the narrator in "The Writing on the Wall." What is the perspective or feeling each is conveying?

SCIENCE

Present Your Work

COLLABORATE

Discuss how you will present your advertisement for a 19th century invention, including any illustrations or photographs you will feature. Use the Presenting Checklist as you practice your presentation. Discuss the sentence starters below and write your answers.

An interesting fact that I learned about the invention is _____

_____

_____

I would like to know more about _____

_____

_____

Quick Tip

The purpose of an advertisement is to persuade readers to take a certain action. As part of your presentation, make sure to point out qualities of the invention that would be likely to attract buyers.

✔ Presenting Checklist

☐ Rehearse your presentation, making sure to present details in a clear, logical order.

☐ Speak slowly, clearly, and with an appropriate volume.

☐ Use an excited expression and convincing tone to "sell" your 19th century invention to your audience.

☐ Make eye contact with your audience.

☐ Listen to comments and questions from the audience and respond politely without interrupting.

Talk About It

? Essential Question

What factors influence how people use money?

There are many ways to take advantage of cost-saving opportunities. The price of an item is just one factor to consider before making a purchase. It's also important to consider how well a product is made and how long it will last. Because prices fluctuate, it's helpful to keep track of prices and plan ahead.

Look at the photograph. Talk to a partner about what you see. Discuss how one can shop and use money wisely. Fill in the chart below with examples.

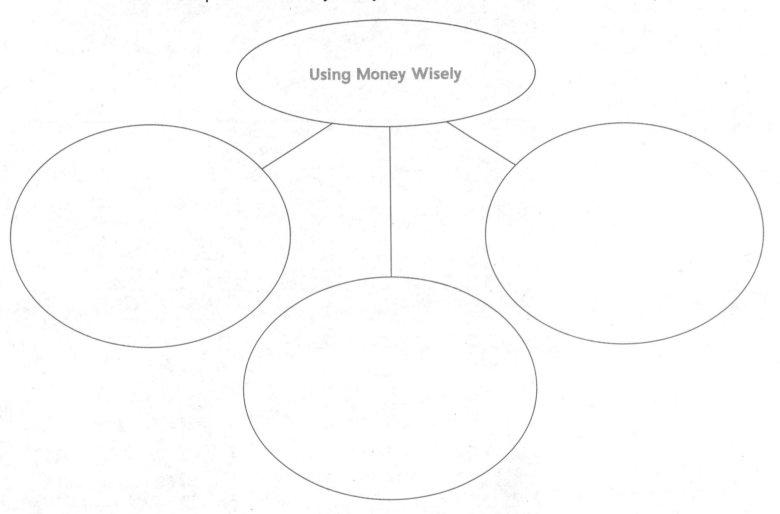

Using Money Wisely

Go online to **my.mheducation.com** and read the "Riches from the Deep" Blast. Think about what people might gain by retrieving sunken ships. Is the risk worth the riches that might be revealed? Blast back your response.

TIME FOR KIDS

TAKE NOTES

Asking questions before you begin to read a text can help you set a purpose for reading. Preview the text by reading the title, headings, and captions. Think about what you already know about money. Then write a question here before you read. Look for answers to your question as you read.

_____

_____

_____

As you read, take note of

Interesting Words _____

_____

_____

_____

Key Details _____

_____

_____

_____

_____

Essential Question

? What factors influence how people use money?

Read how currency has evolved in response to changing needs.

At the U.S. Mint in Philadelphia, these "blanks" will soon become pennies.

Stephen Hilger/Bloomberg via Getty Images

MAKING MONEY
A STORY OF CHANGE

What do cows, sacks of grain, seashells, strings of beads, and swaths of deerskin have in common? They have all been used as money. Currency in the form of coins and bills is a fairly recent development. And before there was any currency at all, there was barter.

Let's Make a Deal

Barter is **basically** a cashless system for exchanging goods or services. People likely bartered from the earliest days of human society. Maybe someone could make tools but needed help hunting. Another person was a good hunter but needed an ax. When they bartered, the toolmaker got help hunting and the hunter got an ax. Today, some believe the give-and-take of bartering is a useful **formula** for exchanges of goods and services, but money makes it easier for us to buy what we need.

How Many Cows Does That Cost?

About 9000 B.C., humans developed agriculture and started living in communities. They grew crops and raised animals for food. So the first form of currency was probably livestock. People could pay for goods and services with cattle, sheep, goats, pigs, or camels. Grain and other crops served as money, too. As societies developed, however, ships and caravans made a growing **inventory** of goods **available** for trade over great distances. Suddenly, big live cows and huge sacks of grain were no longer practical currency. People saw the clear advantage of money that would not die or spoil.

Shopping with Shells

About 1200 B.C., the Chinese began using cowrie shells as money. Cowries are animals that live along many coastlines, so people in Africa

FIND TEXT EVIDENCE

Read

Paragraphs 1–2

Reread

The author says barter came before the use of currency. **Underline** text evidence that helps you understand what barter is.

Paragraphs 3–4

Author's Point of View

What is the author's claim about the use of crops and livestock as currency as societies developed?

_____

_____

_____

Draw a box around text evidence that helped you find your answer.

Reread

Author's Craft

How do the headings help you understand the information that is in the text?

SHARED READ

FIND TEXT EVIDENCE 🔍

Read

Paragraphs 1–2 of
The Advantages of Metal Money

Reread

The author says metal money was more convenient than earlier forms of currency. **Underline** text evidence that explains how metal money developed.

Paragraph 1 of
Paying with Paper Gets Popular

Root Words

Circle the root of *undeniable*. What does *undeniable* mean?

_____

_____

Reread

Author's Craft

Why does the author include the graph that provides information about the average price of gold?

---

and India used this form of currency, too. On the other side of the world, Native Americans made money by stringing beads carved from clamshells. They called their currency *wampum*.

Wampum is made from quahog clams.

The Advantages of Metal Money

The Chinese were the first to use metal for making currency. At first, they cast bronze or copper into shapes that resembled cowrie shells or small tools. These **manufactured** "coins" later became flat and, eventually, round. Before long, the use of round metal coins was adopted in other parts of the world, including Asia Minor, Greece, and Rome. Many early coins were stamped with images of animals, deities, or kings.

Examples of coins from the ancient world

A number of **factors** gave metal coins an advantage over earlier forms of currency. This convenient form of currency lasted a long time, was easily recognized and counted, and had values based on the metals from which coins were made, such as silver and gold.

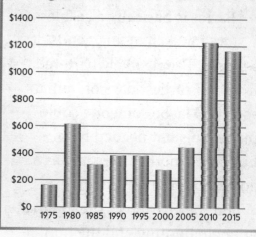

Average price of 1 ounce of gold in U.S. dollars

$1400	
$1200	
$1000	
$800	
$600	
$400	
$200	
$0	1975 1980 1985 1990 1995 2000 2005 2010 2015

Paying with Paper Gets Popular

The Chinese developed yet another form of money about 100 B.C. It was flat, like today's paper money, but each "bill" was actually

(l) Andrew J. Martinez/Science Source; (t, l to r) Silvio Fiore/SuperStock; The Metropolitan Museum of Art, New York, Gift of Joseph H. Durkee, 1899; Ingram Publishing/SuperStock

made of deerskin. In the seventh century A.D., the Chinese began printing the very first paper money. Some 1,400 years later, the usefulness and popularity of lightweight paper bills is undeniable.

More Useful Than Ever

The key idea about money today is that it is issued by governments. In the U.S., your one-dollar bill is worth the same as anyone else's. The same is true for the Chinese *yuan*, the Brazilian *real*, and the *euro* of the European Union. However, the value of one nation's currency in relation to others can **fluctuate** daily.

Today's money is certainly far more versatile than ancient varieties. In addition to exchanging coins and bills, we can write checks that represent the money we have in the bank. We also use electronic, or computer-based, currency. When employers deposit **salaries** directly into their workers' bank accounts, or when we charge an online purchase to a debit or credit card, the exchange is made digitally. From metal to paper to digital currency, each innovative change to money has made it easier for us to purchase what we need.

incamerastock/Alamy

Barter or Bucks?

POINT COUNTERPOINT

Barter Is Better
by Jonah M.

I've learned how to get things I need without spending a dime! Officially, it's called "bartering," but it's as simple as trading what I don't need anymore for something I want. Last week I traded my in-line skates for my friend Robert's guitar. It's a lot like recycling: things you were going to throw away will be used by somebody else. Another way to barter is to trade your time and some work for something you want.

The Case for Cash
by Haylee D.

Cash lets me choose exactly what I want to buy. I can also compare prices of similar items at different stores. I don't always spend my money right away. My mom helped me open a savings account when I was seven years old. Whenever I receive some cash, I go straight to the bank to deposit at least half of it. Over time, the money I save, and any interest it earns, will help me buy things I wouldn't be able to afford otherwise.

Summarize

Use your notes, the graph, and the answers to your questions to summarize how the forms of money have changed over the years.

FIND TEXT EVIDENCE 🔍

Read

Paragraphs 1–2 of More Useful Than Ever
Author's Point of View

Draw a box around the author's claim about money today. **Underline** evidence that supports the claim.

Sidebar

What reasons does Jonah M. give for preferring barter to cash?

_____

_____

_____

Reread

Author's Craft

Why does the author include the sidebar?

Fluency

Take turns reading the final paragraph on page 61 aloud to a partner. Tell your partner if he or she is reading too quickly or too slowly.

Vocabulary

Use the example sentences to talk with a partner about each word. Then answer the questions.

available

Tickets to the concert will be **available** on Friday.

What is an antonym of available?

_____

_____

basically

Although they wear their hair differently, the twins look **basically** the same.

What is a synonym for basically?

_____

_____

factors

People consider such **factors** as type of food and price when choosing a restaurant.

What factors do you consider when choosing a book to read?

_____

_____

fluctuate

The prices of vegetables may **fluctuate** depending on when they are in season.

What causes the outdoor temperature to fluctuate?

_____

_____

formula

The musician's **formula** for success was a combination of lessons and practice.

What is your formula for doing well on a quiz?

_____

_____

Build Your Word List Pick a word you found interesting in the selection you read. Add prefixes and suffixes to make different forms of the root word. Then make a word web with the different forms of the word in your writer's notebook.

inventory

Juan likes to shop when the store gets new **inventory** so he can see the latest styles.

What might be in a store's inventory of school supplies?

_____

_____

_____

manufactured

The gift shop sells **manufactured** goods as well as handmade items.

Name a manufactured product that you use regularly.

_____

_____

_____

salaries

The **salaries** of many workers increase each year to cover rising costs of living.

What happens when salaries decrease?

_____

_____

_____

Root Words

Adding a prefix or a suffix to a word changes the word's meaning. When you read an unfamiliar word, see if you recognize its root. Use that meaning of the root, along with context clues, to identify the unfamiliar word's meaning.

FIND TEXT EVIDENCE

I'm not sure of the meaning of directly *in the last paragraph on page 61. I recognize the letters* -ly *as a suffix, so the root word is* direct. *I know* direct *comes from a Latin root meaning "straight." The phrase* into their workers' bank accounts *provides a context clue. I think* directly *must mean "in a straight way."*

Employers deposit salaries **directly** into their workers' bank accounts.

Your Turn Use root words and context clues to learn the meaning of these words from "Making Money."

relation, *page 61* _____

_____

varieties, *page 61* _____

_____

Reread

Some argumentative texts include details that are difficult to understand at first. You can pause to reread sections of "Making Money: A Story of Change" that are unclear to you.

 FIND TEXT EVIDENCE

You may not be sure why metal coins have been a successful type of currency. Reread paragraph 2 of the section "The Advantages of Metal Money" on page 60.

Page 60

A number of **factors** gave metal coins an advantage over earlier forms of currency. This convenient form of currency lasted a long time, was easily recognized and counted, and had values based on the metals from which coins were made, such as silver and gold.

I read that round metal coins lasted and were "easily recognized and counted." I can infer from this that the advantages of using coins as currency have led people to keep using them even today.

Your Turn Why is it important for governments to issue money? Reread "More Useful Than Ever" on page 61. Remember to use the Reread strategy.

_____

_____

_____

Graphs and Sidebars

"Making Money: A Story of Change" is an argumentative text. An argumentative text presents an author's point of view about a topic. The author supports his or her claims with reasons and may include text features such as graphs, sidebars, and headings.

FIND TEXT EVIDENCE

I can tell "Making Money: A Story of Change" is an argumentative text. It explains why people developed various types of currency throughout history. The bar graph provides further information about an idea discussed in the text. The sidebar provides opinions related to the topic.

Page 60

and India used this form of currency, too. On the other side of the world, Native Americans made money by stringing beads carved from clamshells. They called their currency *wampum*.

Wampum is made from quahog clams.

The Advantages of Metal Money

The Chinese were the first to use metal for making currency. At first, they cast bronze or copper into shapes that resembled cowrie shells or small tools. These **manufactured** "coins" later became flat and, eventually, round. Before long, the use of round metal coins was adopted in other parts of the world, including Asia Minor, Greece, and Rome. Many early coins were stamped with images of animals, deities, or kings.

Examples of coins from the ancient world

A number of **factors** gave metal coins an advantage over earlier forms of currency. This convenient form of currency lasted a long time, was easily recognized and counted, and had values based on the metals from which coins were made, such as silver and gold.

Average price of 1 ounce of gold in U.S. dollars

$1400
$1200
$1000
$800
$600
$400
$200
$0
1975 1980 1985 1990 1995 2000 2005 2010 2015

Paying with Paper Gets Popular

The Chinese developed yet another form of money about 100 B.C. It was flat, like today's paper money, but each "bill" was actually

Graphs

Graphs may support and expand on information in the text and present data visually.

Sidebars

Sidebars provide more information related to the topic.

Your Turn Analyze the sidebar on page 61. How do the titles help you set a purpose for reading?

_____

_____

_____

_____

_____

_____

Author's Point of View

Quick Tip

Pay attention to the author's word choice in an argumentative text. Words such as *useful* or *advantage* point to a specific point of view.

In an argumentative text, the **author's point of view** is the claim the author makes about a topic. Strong claims are supported by reasons and evidence. An author can include facts, or statements that can be proven, to support the claim. Authors may also support a claim with examples or opinions.

 FIND TEXT EVIDENCE

When I reread "Making Money: A Story of Change," I can identify the author's point of view by looking for important facts, examples, and opinions included in each section. I can determine how they support the author's main points and reveal his or her point of view on the topic.

Details	Author's Point of View
Most people today use money instead of bartering.	The author believes that changes to money have made today's currencies more versatile and better able to serve people than ever before.
Livestock as currency became impractical.	
Metal coins had advantages over earlier currency.	
Many forms of currency are available today.	

Your Turn Reread "The Case for Cash" on page 61. Identify the key details and list them in the graphic organizer on page 67. Then state the author's point of view.

Details	Author's Point of View

Respond to Reading

COLLABORATE

Discuss the prompt below. Think about the text features the author uses to help you understand key details and claims in "Making Money: A Story of Change." Use your notes and graphic organizer.

How does the author help you understand how forms of money evolved over time?

_____

_____

_____

_____

_____

_____

_____

_____

_____

_____

_____

_____

Quick Tip

Use these sentence starters to discuss the text and to organize ideas.

- *The headings tell . . .*
- *The author gives specific ideas in order to . . .*
- *Another text feature the author uses is . . .*

Grammar Connections

As you write your response, use present tense verbs when talking about the argumentative text. For example:

The author also uses . . .

The captions give . . .

The author divides . . .

The present tense often communicates more than simple present time. It can also help you convey a general fact.

Generate and Clarify Questions

A good way to focus research is to **generate and clarify questions** about a topic. Clarifying your initial questions can help you more easily locate useful information and understand complex ideas.

For example, if you were to research the Great Depression, you might ask, "What happened during the Great Depression?" This question has many possible responses, and it isn't clear what type of responses, or answers, you are looking for. You need to clarify what you are asking. For example, asking a question about the effect of the Great Depression on employment will provide you with more specific information.

What is another example of a clarifying question that you can ask about the Great Depression?

COLLABORATE

Write a News Report With a group, research an economic downturn in U.S. history, such as the Great Depression, Black Monday, or the 2008 financial crisis. Then write a news report about the downturn. To prepare, create a list of questions you want to answer. For example:

- What caused the economic collapse?
- What effects did it have on people?
- How did the government try to resolve the issue?
- How successful were the government's efforts?

Discuss what reliable current and historical sources you might use in your research and what images or other visual aids might be helpful to display. You will share your news report with your classmates.

> Follow these tips to write a compelling news report:
> - Include a heading that summarizes the event.
> - Explain who, what, where, when, and why in the first paragraph of your report.
> - Provide more specific details in additional paragraphs.
> - Use vivid language and quotations to keep your audience engaged.

The Economic Roller Coaster

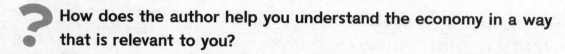 **How does the author help you understand the economy in a way that is relevant to you?**

Literature Anthology: pages 50–53

 Talk About It Reread the first two paragraphs on **Literature Anthology** page 51. Talk about why the author uses real life examples to help you understand the topic.

Cite Text Evidence How does the author make the information relevant to you?

Text Evidence	How Is This Relevant?

Write The author's real-life examples help me understand that the economy _____

_____

How does the author use text features to help you understand supply and demand?

 Talk About It Look at the text features on **Literature Anthology** pages 52–53. Talk with a partner about new information you learned and why the author includes the features.

Cite Text Evidence How do the text features help you understand supply and demand? Write the name of each text feature at the top of each column, then say how it helped you understand supply and demand below.

Write Text features help me understand supply and demand by _____

_____

_____

_____

Quick Tip

Some diagrams use symbols to represent objects, people, or actions. To understand this kind of diagram, identify the symbols it uses. Then make sure you know what each symbol means.

 Evaluate Information

The writer of the sidebar on page 53 believes the government does not need to influence supply and demand. Think about the reasons or evidence that support the claim. Is the argument convincing? Do you agree?

Respond to Reading

COLLABORATE Discuss the prompt below. Apply your own knowledge about supply and demand to inform your answer. Use your notes and graphic organizer.

How does the sidebar help you understand a different point of view about the free-market economy in America?

_____

_____

_____

_____

_____

_____

_____

_____

_____

_____

_____

_____

Quick Tip

Use these sentence starters to talk about and cite text evidence.

- *The author of the sidebar believes . . .*
- *I read that . . .*
- *This helps me understand . . .*

Self-Selected Reading

Choose a text and fill in your writer's notebook with the title, author, and genre of the text. Include a personal response to the text in your writer's notebook.

Our Federal Reserve at Work

Literature Anthology: pages 54–55

1   Likewise, lower interest rates provide reasons for people to borrow more and save less. A low interest rate is likely to cause businesses to invest more and expand. It will also encourage people to make more purchases. In this way, interest rates affect how much economic activity takes place in an economy.

2   I believe that when the economy slows down the Federal Reserve must take action. It should lower interest rates and keep money moving through the economic system. I also believe the Fed should raise interest rates if people start borrowing too much.

3   The flow chart below helps explain this sound monetary position.

Reread paragraphs 1 and 2. **Underline** clues that help you understand the author's opinion about what the Federal Reserve should do. Then go back and **circle** evidence that supports the author's point of view.

Reread paragraph 3 and look at the diagram. **Draw a box** around a clue the author uses to persuade you to feel as he or she does.

COLLABORATE

Talk with a partner about how the text evidence and diagram work together to inform you about the economy and the author's opinion.

Low interest rates

% Healthy economy keeps interest rates low

More money to spend

More spending

More jobs to make products

More demand for products

Allied Supplies

The **Ripple** Effect
When the cost of borrowing money is at the right level, the entire economy runs smoothly.

? **How does the author persuade you to agree with his or her opinions about the Federal Reserve?**

Talk About It Reread the excerpt on page 73. Discuss with a partner how the author states his or her opinions.

Cite Text Evidence What does the author say to persuade you to agree? Write text evidence in the chart.

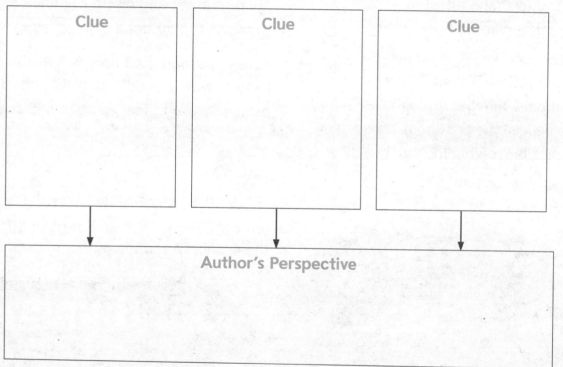

Clue	Clue	Clue

↓   ↓   ↓

Author's Perspective

Write The author persuades me to agree with him or her by _____

_____

_____

Cause and Effect

It's often useful to organize ideas in an argumentative text by using cause-and-effect relationships. An author can support his or her argument by explaining what causes an event to happen and its effect on other events.

FIND TEXT EVIDENCE

On **Literature Anthology** page 55, the author discusses what happens when interest rates are too high. The word *because* is a clue that the author is stating a cause (paying back a loan costs too much when interest rates are high) and a consequential effect (people are not likely to borrow money).

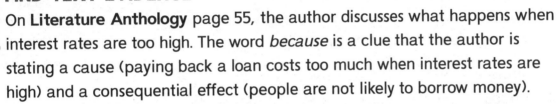

When interest rates become too high, however, businesses and people are not likely to borrow money from a bank. This is because it will cost them too much to pay it back.

Your Turn Reread the rest of **Literature Anthology** page 55.

• What cause-and-effect relationship does the author use to discuss lower interest rates? _____

_____

• How does the author's use of cause and effect support the argument about how the Federal Reserve should act? _____

_____

Readers to Writers

When you use cause-and-effect relationships to organize your writing, include signal words and phrases that help readers distinguish between causes and effects.

• To signal a **cause**, use *because, since, resulted from,* or *due to.*

• To signal an **effect**, try *therefore, as a result, consequently,* or *for this reason.*

Text Connections

? How does the marketplace in the painting contribute to your understanding of the free market discussed in *The Economic Roller Coaster* and "Our Federal Reserve at Work"?

Talk About It Look at the painting and read the caption. Talk with a partner about how supply and demand as discussed in *The Economic Roller Coaster* could impact the vendors in the painting.

Cite Text Evidence **Circle** examples in the painting of a free market economy. In the caption, **underline** text evidence that supports your discussion.

Write The painting deepens my understanding of the free market by _____

_____

_____

_____

_____

_____

_____

_____

Flemish painter Pieter Angellis created this oil on copper painting of Covent Garden around 1726. Covent Garden is located in London's West End and has housed a fruit and vegetable market off and on since the 1600s.

Accuracy and Rate

To read an argumentative text with **accuracy**, think about how to pronounce statistical information like dates and percentages. Also, look for punctuation clues that indicate how you should adjust your **rate**, or speed.

Page 59

About 9000 B.C., humans developed agriculture and started living in communities. They grew crops and raised animals for food. So the first form of currency was probably livestock. People could pay for goods and services with cattle, sheep, goats, pigs, or camels.

Think about how you might read a date differently than you would a number.

Commas separating items in a series tell you to pause slightly after reading each item.

Your Turn Turn to pages 60-61 of "Making Money: A Story of Change." With a partner, take turns reading "Paying with Paper Gets Popular" aloud. Focus on reading dates written in numeric form as accurately as those written as words. Look for punctuation that can inform your reading rate.

Afterward, think about how you did. Complete these sentences.

I remembered to _____

_____

Next time, I will _____

_____

Expert Model

Literature Anthology: pages 50–53

Features of an Opinion Essay

An opinion essay is a form of argumentative text. It states and supports the author's point of view about a particular topic. An opinion essay

- introduces a clearly stated opinion, or claim, using a formal style of writing;

- supports the claim with reasons, facts, and relevant evidence;

- often includes an opposing opinion and then argues against it.

Analyze an Expert Model Studying argumentative texts will help you learn how to plan and write an opinion essay. **Reread** the section "If You Ask Me . . ." in *The Economic Roller Coaster* on page 53 in the **Literature Anthology**. Write your answers to the questions below.

What claim does the author make about the government taking actions to help the economy? _____

_____

What words or phrases indicate that the author is stating an opinion?

_____

_____

Plan: Choose Your Topic

Brainstorm With a partner, talk about the difference between shopping in a retail store versus online. What do you know about each experience? What are the benefits and drawbacks of each? Write your ideas on the lines below.

_____

_____

_____

_____

_____

Writing Prompt Decide whether you think there are more benefits to shopping for goods and services online or in a physical store. Then write an essay that states your opinion supported by reasons and evidence. In your essay, be sure to address an opposing opinion and refute it using evidence.

I will write about _____.

Purpose and Audience Think about your purpose for writing and the people who will be reading your opinion essay.

My purpose is to _____.

My audience will be _____.

Plan In your writer's notebook, make an Opinion web to plan your writing. Fill in the center oval with your opinion, or claim.

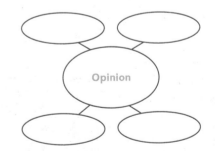

Plan: Strong Introduction

Quick Tip

Think about what you do when you meet someone for the first time. You are probably friendly and polite. The introduction to your essay should do the same. Use language that is respectful to introduce your topic and state your opinion.

Write an Effective Introduction The introduction of an opinion essay offers the chance to identify your topic and state your claim. An effective introduction makes your position on an issue immediately clear to readers. It often includes an interesting fact or surprising statistic that grabs the reader's attention and makes him or her eager to read more. As you plan and write your introduction, think about these questions:

• How can I clearly identify the topic of my opinion essay?

• How should I state my opinion, or claim?

• What statistics or other facts will grab my readers' attention?

List two facts you could include in your introduction.

1 _____

2 _____

 Graphic Organizer Once you have gathered information to support your claim, fill in the rest of your web. If you need more space to write your details, use a separate sheet of paper in your writer's notebook.

Digital Tools

For more information about how to write for an audience, watch "Write for Your Audience." Go to **my.mheducation.com**.

Draft

Relevant Evidence An author uses relevant details to support his or her claims. Facts, details, statistics, examples, and quotations connected to the topic are all types of relevant evidence. In the example from "Making Money: A Story of Change" below, notice how the author's evidence supports his claim that he can get what he needs from bartering.

> I've learned how to get things I need without spending a dime! Officially, it's called "bartering," but it's as simple as trading what I don't need anymore for something I want. Last week I traded my in-line skates for my friend Robert's guitar.

Now use the example above as a model to write a paragraph for your opinion essay. Make sure your evidence is relevant and supports your claim.

_____

_____

_____

_____

_____

Write a Draft Use your graphic organizer to help you write your draft in your writer's notebook. Don't forget to write a strong introduction that identifies your topic and states your claim. In the body of your essay, support your opinion with at least two reasons and relevant evidence, along with an opposing argument and evidence that refutes it.

Revise

Logical Order Using a logical order to organize your opinion essay helps readers make sense of your ideas. Read the paragraph below. Then revise it so that the information is logically presented. Add transitions to clarify the relationships between the claim, reasons, and opposing argument.

> It's true that you might have more choices if you shop online.
> You might be disappointed in your purchase when it arrives. There is no substitute for actually touching and feeling something you want to buy. That's impossible to do if you are shopping online.

_____

_____

_____

_____

_____

_____

_____

Revision Now revise your draft of your opinion essay. Make sure your claim and the reasons and evidence you use to support it are presented in a logical order. Use transitions to connect your ideas.

Peer Conferences

COLLABORATE

Review a Draft Listen carefully as a partner reads his or her work aloud. Take notes about what you liked and what was difficult to follow. Begin by telling what you liked about the draft. Ask questions that will help the writer think more about the writing. Make suggestions that you think will make the writing stronger. Use the sentence starters below.

I was convinced by this part of your argument because . . .

You could add more relevant evidence by . . .

I have a question about . . .

To organize your evidence more logically, you could . . .

Partner Feedback After your partner gives you feedback on your draft, write one of the suggestions that you will use in your revision. Refer to the rubric on page 85 as you give feedback.

Based on my partner's feedback, I will _____

_____

_____

After you finish giving each other feedback, reflect on the peer conference. What was helpful? What might you do differently next time?

Revision As you revise your draft, use the Revising Checklist to help you figure out what text you may need to move, elaborate on, or delete. Remember to use the rubric on page 85 to help you with your revision.

Revising Checklist

☐ Does my writing fit my purpose and audience?

☐ Do I have a strong introduction that identifies the topic and clearly states my claim?

☐ Have I included enough relevant evidence to support my claim?

☐ Do I order my reasons and evidence logically and use transitions to connect ideas?

☐ Have I addressed an opposing argument and provided evidence to refute it?

Tech Tip

If you read your partner's work on a computer or tablet, use digital sticky notes or the commenting tool to note feedback. Use different colors to highlight sentences you liked and those that require revision.

Edit and Proofread

When you **edit** and **proofread** your writing, you look for and correct mistakes in spelling, punctuation, capitalization, and grammar. Reading through a revised draft multiple times can help you make sure you're correcting any errors. Use the checklist below to edit your sentences.

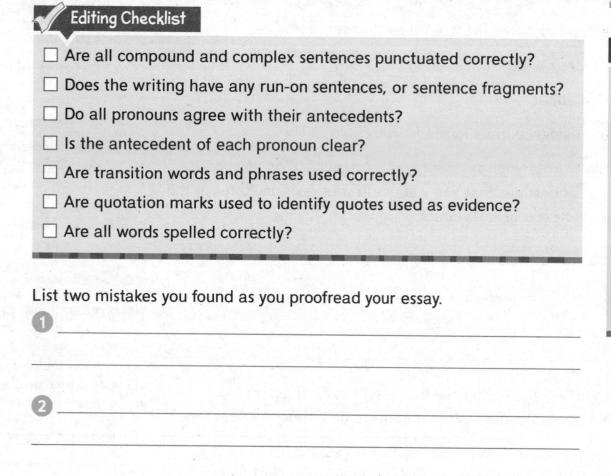

✔ Editing Checklist

☐ Are all compound and complex sentences punctuated correctly?

☐ Does the writing have any run-on sentences, or sentence fragments?

☐ Do all pronouns agree with their antecedents?

☐ Is the antecedent of each pronoun clear?

☐ Are transition words and phrases used correctly?

☐ Are quotation marks used to identify quotes used as evidence?

☐ Are all words spelled correctly?

List two mistakes you found as you proofread your essay.

1 _____

_____

2 _____

_____

Tech Tip

Grammar checkers are helpful tools, but they are not perfect. Be thoughtful before accepting any changes a grammar checker suggests.

Grammar Connections

As you edit and proofread, make sure you punctuate compound and complex sentences correctly. In compound sentences, a comma should go before the coordinating conjunction (*and, or, but, yet, so*) that joins the two independent clauses. A comma should follow introductory clauses in complex sentences.

Publish, Present, and Evaluate

Publishing When you **publish** your writing, you create a clean, neat final copy that is free of mistakes. If you decide to print, leave the space of a pencil point between letters and the space of a pencil between words. Consider adding graphs, photographs, or other visuals to help make your opinion essay more persuasive and engaging.

Presentation When you are ready to **present** your work, rehearse your presentation. Use the Presenting Checklist to help you.

Evaluate After you publish your writing, use the rubric below to **evaluate** your writing.

What did you do successfully? _____

What needs more work? _____

_____

4	3	2	1
• clearly introduces an opinion about the topic	• introduces an opinion about the topic	• does not clearly introduce an opinion about the topic	• does not introduce an opinion about the topic
• presents reasons and relevant evidence in a logical order to support the claim	• presents reasons and relevant evidence in a mostly logical order to support the claim	• presents reasons and mostly relevant evidence, but not in logical order	• presents no reasons or evidence relevant to the support the claim
• addresses an opposing argument and refutes it with sufficient evidence	• addresses an opposing argument and refutes it with some evidence	• addresses an opposing argument, but does not use evidence to refute it	• does not address an opposing argument

Spiral Review

You have learned new skills and strategies in Unit 1 that will help you read more critically. Now it is time to practice what you have learned.

- Context Clues
- Author's Point of View
- Root Words
- Main Idea
- Narrator
- Character, Setting, Plot
- Metaphors
- Make Inferences

Connect to Content

- Research a Topic
- Conduct an Interview

Read the selection and choose the best answer to each question.

Allowances for Kids:
THE GREAT DEBATE

[1] Adults in your family make very important decisions that impact you every day. At some point, one decision might have to do with whether you should receive an allowance. Some adults believe that giving their child money on a regular basis helps him or her develop good financial skills. Their kids might get an allowance for doing chores or for maintaining good grades or good behavior. Or, the kids might not have to do anything to get an allowance. Other adults choose not to give their children an allowance because they see absolutely no benefit in it.

LESSONS IN FINANCE

[2] Proponents of giving an allowance state that having their own money helps kids learn financial literacy. Financial literacy is the ability to manage money wisely. Studies have shown that kids who manage their own money gain greater self-esteem, put more thought into how they spend their money, and learn the importance of saving money. Many families help their kids set up bank accounts. They also guide their kids on how to budget for new purchases.

[3] Of course, there are two sides to the debate. Some financial experts point to studies that show little evidence that students learn by having an allowance. In addition, they insist that gaining financial literacy as a young person doesn't always lead to smart decisions about money later in life. And some people believe that giving teens an allowance spoils them and leaves them believing they're entitled to the money. They also fear that teens will spend their money on foolish things.

Opinion: Allowance should not be used as a reward.

4   Children in the United States have earned allowances for many years—likely since the time of the Industrial Revolution. Today, more than 50 percent of U.S. children receive an allowance. Yet some issues are still debated. For example, should kids be paid simply for being a member of a family? Should earning an allowance be tied to receiving good grades in school? Or should an allowance be related to specific chores done to help the family? There are <u>infinite</u> opinions on these questions and on the kinds of things kids should be allowed to purchase with their allowance.

5   Studies have shown that receiving money for completing tasks, such as watching younger siblings or keeping one's room clean, is a poor idea. Proponents of this view believe that rewarding kids for doing everyday chores sends the wrong message. After all, helping out in a family should simply be considered good citizenship. And to give an allowance for getting good grades seems even worse. That's because working hard and trying to achieve one's best should be natural goals that help kids work toward being successful adults.

6   To give or not to give an allowance will likely remain a controversial topic. Yet there may be a middle ground in the debate. Some financial experts once believed that an allowance helped teach financial literacy. But they were surprised to discover that the financial knowledge individuals gained as teens didn't always continue to adulthood. Examining the evidence leads to an important conclusion: unless families spend time discussing how to manage one's money, receiving an allowance teaches very little, and using allowance as a reward is a bad idea. Unless teens are faced with the consequences of monetary decisions, they don't learn financial literacy skills. It seems right to conclude that allowances should be accompanied by frequent family discussions, a sense of responsibility, and real consequences.

SHOW WHAT YOU LEARNED

1 What is the main idea of paragraph 1?

   A Financial literacy is an important skill.

   B Adults have differing opinions on giving children an allowance.

   C It is important for kids to receive an allowance.

   D Adults must make important decisions for their children.

2 The word <u>proponents</u> in paragraph 2 means —

   F opponents

   G creators

   H supporters

   J protestors

3 The word <u>infinite</u> comes from the Latin root <u>fin</u> meaning "end." In paragraph 4, what does <u>infinite</u> mean?

   A endless

   B finished

   C recurring

   D ending

4 In paragraph 5, the author supports the claim that allowance should not be used as a reward by —

   F showing how allowance improves financial literacy

   G describing how kids spend their money

   H providing the number of kids who recieve an allowance

   J citing studies about allowance

Quick Tip

For multiple-choice questions, rule out the answers that are definitely wrong. Then spend some time focusing on the remaining answers.

Read the selection and choose the best answer to each question.

Not So Bad After All

1　"I'm not going to Grandma's house," bellowed José at his mom. "Not for a day, not for a week, and definitely not for the whole blazing-hot summer."

2　"You'll be fine. The summer will fly by in Mérida at your grandma's house. Spending some time in Mexico will be fun."

3　"Come on, Mami, all my friends are staying here in Chicago," José argued. "I already signed up for the summer basketball league. And my friends are counting on me. I'm their star point guard!"

4　"I'm sure you'll be able to pick up a basketball game or two with your cousins while you are away. Getting to know you means so much to your grandma. After all, she hasn't seen you in person since you were a little boy. And you might just learn something about where our family is from."

5　"Mami, Grandma sees me every week on the computer," José grumbled. "And it's hard enough talking with her then. Imagine how bad I'll feel struggling with my baby Spanish. Forget it, I'm not going."

6　"You can whine all you want, José. But you're spending the summer with Grandma. End of story."

7　Boiling mad, José turned and stomped his way outside to the driveway where his basketball hoop was set up. He dribbled toward it and tried to calm his anger by focusing on shooting baskets. After a good long while, he stopped, took a deep breath, and faced the brutal reality. "Mexico, here I come," he grumbled under his breath.

8   José knew the fight was futile. After all, his mom had already purchased his plane ticket. And another bitter fact: she'd already committed to teaching a summer course in Boston. So there would be no one to stay with him in Chicago anyway.

9   "I'm stuck—plain and simple," he said, angrily stomping back inside and up to his room. He plopped down at his desk and absentmindedly surfed the Internet. "If I'm going to Mérida, I might as well see what the place is about," he thought. As he clicked from site to site, one photograph caught his eye. He found himself looking at a photo of ancient walls surrounding a large grass playing field. Near the top of two of the walls a large stone ring was sticking out.

10 He read the caption: *A perfect day trip from Mérida, Chichén Itzá is one of the most important examples of an ancient Maya city. This huge ball court is a stunning remnant of the city.*

11 "Ball courts? Mami must have somehow bookmarked this page," José thought. "She'll do anything to get me to pipe down about going away." But he couldn't resist reading on.

12 He learned that more than 1,500 ball courts have been discovered in Mesoamerica, in what is now part of Mexico and Central America. This game was played with heavy solid rubber balls, and the rules of the game varied from place to place. In some places, players tried to get the ball through the rings on the walls. The largest known ball court is in Chichén Itzá.

13 José looked up, amazed that the passion for ball games was so ancient. He wondered if any of his ancestors had been players. He thought for a minute and then yelled downstairs. "Hey Mami, do you think Grandma might take me to Chichén Itzá?"

Ralf Broskvar/Shutterstock

1 Who narrates the story?

A an outside narrator

B José

C José's mom

D José's grandma

2 Which statement best summarizes the story's conflict?

F José wants to spend the summer at home.

G José's mom has to teach in Boston.

H José does not think he will like Mérida.

J José does not speak Spanish well.

3 Which words from the story include a metaphor?

A ". . . calm his anger by focusing on shooting baskets."

B ". . . amazed that the passion for ball games was so ancient."

C "Boiling mad, José turned and stomped his way outside . . ."

D "So there would be no one to stay with him in Chicago anyway."

4 How does reading about Chichén Itzá change José's feelings?

F He wishes he could stay in Chicago.

G He thinks about talking with his grandma in Spanish.

H He decides to play more basketball.

J He realizes it might be fun to go to Mexico.

COMPARING GENRES

COLLABORATE

- In the **Literature Anthology,** reread the narrative nonfiction *Into the Volcano* on pages 10–23 and the biographical article "Donna O'Meara: The Volcano Lady" on pages 26–29.

- Use the Venn diagram below to show how the narrative written by Donna O'Meara is similar to and different from the biographical article about her. Thinking about genre characteristics will help you compare and contrast the two different genres.

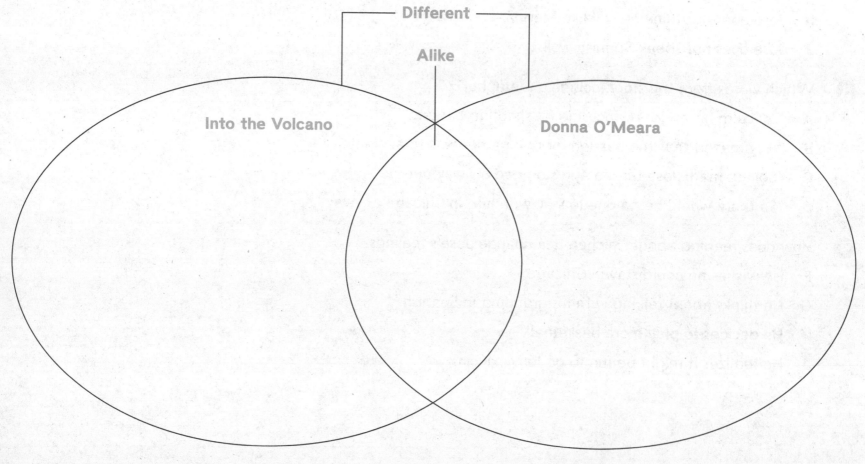

Different

Alike

Into the Volcano

Donna O'Meara

WORD ORIGINS

COLLABORATE

Many English words have origins in other languages, such as Greek or Latin. Knowing the meanings of common Greek and Latin **root words** can help you figure out the meanings of unfamiliar words.

- When you read an unfamiliar word, see if you recognize its root. If you are unsure, look up the word in an online or print dictionary that includes information about the origin of words.

- Complete the chart below by adding the origin of each root listed in the first column. Then search for two or more examples of words that contain each root. Add your examples to the chart. Then use each example in a sentence in your writer's notebook. Use a dictionary for help.

Root Word	Meaning	Origin	Example	Additional Examples
ped	"foot"		pedal	
cent	"hundred"		centipede	
bi	"two"		bicycle	
ism	"result of"		activism	
graph	"writing"		autograph	
form	"shape"		formation	
cycl	"circle"		unicycle	

petrow/iStock/Getty Images

RESEARCH A TOPIC

COLLABORATE

SCIENCE

In *Into the Volcano,* you read about Surtsey, a volcanic island off the coast of Iceland. Surtsey was an undersea volcano that grew slowly until it reached the surface of the ocean, forming a new island.

- Research Surtsey. Ask focused questions to find information about how and when the island was formed, how it got its name, and what kinds of wildlife are present on the island.

- Use print and online sources to answer your questions and record your notes in a chart like the one below. Include at least one primary source—such as a quote from a researcher—and at least two secondary sources. Use your notes to plan your draft. Edit your work and share your findings with a partner.

Underwater volcanic activity created Surtsey, an island off Iceland's southern coast.

Research Question	Answer	Source/Type of Source

CONDUCT AN INTERVIEW

You've probably read dozens of interviews or seen them on TV. But have you ever thought about what goes into conducting a great interview? Read these tips to improve your own interviewing skills:

- Good interviewers ask questions that elicit interesting responses. Avoid asking questions that will lead to one-word responses such as *yes* or *no*. The more specific your questions are, the more interesting your interviewee's answers will be.

- Listen carefully to the response. Paying close attention to what your interviewee says can lead to great follow-up questions. Also, it will help you avoid asking a question about a topic that was already discussed.

Volcano expert Donna O'Meara

- Read the chart to see examples of good and bad interview questions.

Do Ask. . .	Don't Ask. . .
What surprised you most about _____? Why? How do you plan for_____? What advice can you give to others who want to study geology?	• How old are you? • Do you usually get tired? • How many hours do you work each day?

Imagine you have the opportunity to interview Donna O'Meara. What questions would you ask? Write three questions you would ask about her life and work and record them below.

1 _____

2 _____

3 _____

Stefanie Keenan/WireImage/Getty Images

WHAT DID YOU LEARN?

Use the rubric to evaluate yourself on the skills you learned in this unit.
Write your scores in the boxes below.

4	3	2	1
I can successfully identify all examples of this skill.	I can identify most examples of this skill.	I can identify a few examples of this skill.	I need to work more on this skill.

☐ Main Idea and Details   ☐ Character, Setting, Plot   ☐ Author's Point of View

☐ Metaphors and Similes   ☐ Context Clues   ☐ Root Words

Something that I need to work more on is _____ because

_____

_____

_____

Text to Self Think back over the texts that you have read in this unit.
Choose one text and write a short paragraph explaining a personal
connection that you have made to the text.

I made a personal connection to _____ because _____

_____

_____

_____

_____

Present Your Work

COLLABORATE

Discuss with your group how you will present your news report. Use the Presenting Checklist as you practice your news report. Discuss the sentence starters below and write your answers.

An interesting fact I learned about the economy is _____

_____

_____

I would like to know more about _____

_____

_____

Tech Tip

Consider recording a live video presentation of your news report. Assign roles (director, anchor, camera operator, and so on) to members of your group. Rehearse your report before you go "live" to make sure all group members understand their specific task.

Presenting Checklist

☐ Rehearse your news report as a group. Ask for feedback from other group members.

☐ Use formal language in your news report.

☐ Speak slowly and clearly. Use appropriate tone and expression.

☐ Speak directly to your viewers, whether you are filming the report or presenting it live.

☐ Look at the camera if you are filming your news report. If not, make eye contact with people in the audience.

Talk About It

The photograph shows the remains of the Bouleuterion, a building constructed around 175 B.C. in the ancient Ionian city of Priene. The people of Priene governed themselves. The Bouleuterion was a place for the council to meet and decide important issues, much like the United States Senate chamber is today.

Talk to your partner about what you have learned about Priene's government from both the text and photograph. Write your ideas in the web.

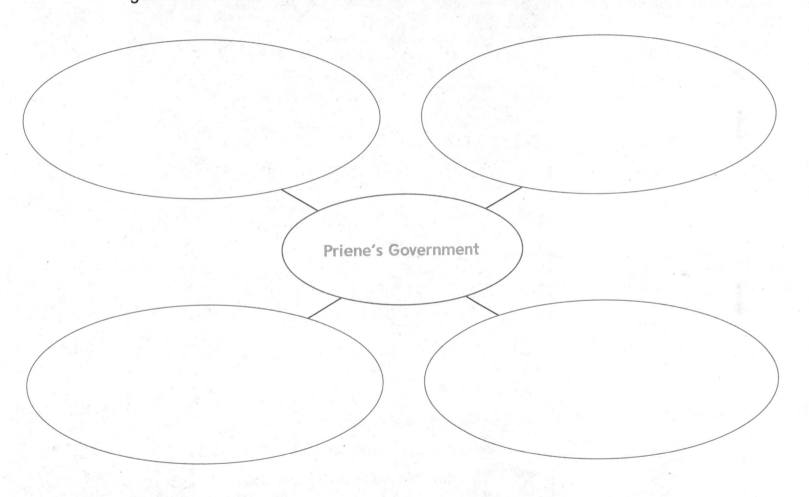

Priene's Government

Go online to **my.mheducation.com** and read the "A Site for the People" Blast. Do you think that all citizens should have a say in political decisions? Think about why democracies need public gathering places. Then blast back your response.

Vanni/Art Resource

TAKE NOTES

Setting a purpose, or thinking about what you hope to learn, will help you focus on important information in the text. Preview the headings, photos, and text features. What do you hope to learn? Write your purpose for reading.

_____

_____

_____

As you read, take note of

Interesting Words _____

_____

_____

_____

Key Details _____

_____

_____

_____

The Democracy DEBATE

Essential Question

? **How did democracy develop?**

Read about the ideas that philosophers in ancient Greece and Rome had about democracy.

Left page: Ocean/Corbis; Right page: (bkgd) Siede Preis/Getty Images; (t) Hans Laubel/iStock/Getty Images; (b) DEA/G. DAGLI ORTI/De Agostini Picture Library/Getty Images

Born and Raised in Greece

Have you ever heard the phrase "government by the people?" That is the meaning of the word *democracy*. The United States is a democratic republic, as are many countries around the world. But where did democracy come from? Some of the earliest ideas about democracy arose in the city of Athens in ancient Greece. But how should democracy be put into practice? The answer to that question has been strongly debated for centuries.

Even when democracy was a new idea, people argued about how it should work. How should power be shared? Should *all* people be allowed to vote and make important decisions? Among the first people to think about these key issues were the ancient Greek philosophers.

Great Minds

The word *philosopher* means "lover of wisdom," a person who seeks knowledge and is able to make good and fair decisions. One of the best-known Greek philosophers, Socrates, lived nearly 2,500 years ago. He valued wisdom highly, and he thought deeply about

Socrates

democracy. Socrates was one of the **principal** critics of government run by the people. He felt that only fair and wise individuals should be allowed to decide things.

The ideas that Socrates had about democracy were considered dangerous to the existing democracy in Athens. The Athenian leaders did not want some other "fair and wise" people **aspiring** to run their city. Socrates was a famous teacher. And **speculation** among the city's leaders included worries that he would encourage young students to pick up his radical ideas. So they chose to execute him.

Students of Philosophy

The philosopher Plato had studied with Socrates. He also thought seriously about democracy. In 380 B.C., Plato shared his ideas about government in his book *The Republic*. He agreed with Socrates that rule by the people would bring

FIND TEXT EVIDENCE

Read

Paragraph 1

Ask and Answer Questions

What question does the author ask and answer in this paragraph?

_____

_____

Underline text evidence that helps you answer the question.

Paragraphs 2–5

Make Inferences

Circle Socrates's views. **Draw a box** around the Athenian leaders' views. What can you infer about Athenian leaders?

_____

_____

Reread

Author's Craft

Why do you think the author titled this text "The Democracy Debate"?

Read

Paragraph 1 (First Full Paragraph)

Compare and Contrast

How did Aristotle's views on democracy differ from Socrates's?

_____

_____

Paragraphs 2–3

Ask and Answer Questions

Write a question you can ask and answer about Cicero. **Underline** the answer in the text.

_____

_____

Reread

Author's Craft

How does the author help you understand that people's views of democracy changed over time?

about poor decisions and a weak government. But, unlike his teacher, he believed that three different groups of people could share the responsibility of governing. The "highest" group would be philosopher-kings guided only by what is best for the state. The second group would be soldiers who protected the state. The last group would be common people who provided goods and services.

Around 388 B.C., Plato formed a school called the Academy. A star pupil there was the philosopher Aristotle, who believed in balance and moderation. About 350 B.C., Aristotle wrote in his book *Politics* that a government that tries to **restrict** power to a few educated men would not work. It would benefit only the rich. A democracy run by common people would not work either, because such people might not make wise decisions.

Philosopher Kings

Soldiers

Producers of Goods and Services

Aristotle's solution was combining the two. This would give people from all parts of society a voice.

Aristotle

Changes in Rome

About 300 years after Aristotle, the influence of Greek thinking was still felt by philosophers in Rome. Cicero is the best known Roman philosopher. Like Aristotle, he believed a balance of power brought peace and prosperity. That was because different types of people took part in government.

Cicero believed that the Roman republic was the best model for government because it was mixed. It combined features of a monarchy, an aristocracy, and a democracy. Cicero saw that the Roman republic was breaking down, mostly because the aristocracy had gained too much power. In his book, *On the Republic*, he urged a return to a more balanced government.

Cicero

(tc) DEA PICTURE LIBRARY/Getty Images; (tr, c, bl) Siede Preis/Getty Images; (br) ALESSANDRO VANNINI/Corbis Historical/Getty Images

Philosopher	Place	Time Period	Ideas About Democracy
Socrates	Greece	469–399 B.C.	Only wise and just people should govern.
Plato	Greece	427–347 B.C.	Rule should be shared by philosopher-kings, soldiers, and providers of goods.
Aristotle	Greece	384–322 B.C.	Educated and common people should each have a role in government.
Cicero	Rome	106–43 B.C.	The Roman republic—a monarch, an aristocracy, and the people—is best.

The Debate Continues

The founders of the United States also thought about how a democracy should be organized. They studied governments that had **preceded** ours and believed that the **foundation** of any new government should revisit Greek and Roman ideas. For example, Thomas Paine wrote booklets to **promote** the idea that people should govern themselves. James Madison admired Aristotle's and Cicero's beliefs in balancing power among different groups.

In 1787, Madison helped Alexander Hamilton write a set of essays called *The Federalist* to encourage states to ratify the Constitution. They made the case for having a *pair* of law-making groups. The smaller Senate would be similar to Rome's senate, while the House of Representatives would give more people a voice. They also endorsed having one president and a system of courts to interpret the laws.

Today, people are still debating what the meaning of *democracy* is and how our government should be organized. The U.S. Constitution has been amended more than 25 times to reflect changing ideas. Yet it is important to remember that our government has roots in ideas from ancient times. Democracy has **withstood** the test of time.

Summarize

Use your notes, the diagram, and the chart to write a summary of the different ideas people have had about democracy over the centuries.

FIND TEXT EVIDENCE

Read

Charts

How does the chart clarify information in the text?

_____

_____

_____

Paragraph 1

Greek and Latin Prefixes

The prefix *re-* means "back" or "again." What does *revisit* mean?

_____

Paragraphs 2–3

Compare and Contrast

To what does the author compare Madison's and Hamilton's idea for a Senate? **Underline** the answer.

Reread

Author's Craft

Why do you think the author tells how many times the U.S. Constitution has been amended?

Vocabulary

Use the example sentences to talk with a partner about each word. Then answer the questions.

aspiring

At the tryouts, we heard many singers who were **aspiring** to perform in our school talent show.

What is a synonym for aspiring?

_____

_____

foundation

Learning to dribble the ball is a good **foundation** for playing basketball.

What is a foundation for playing baseball?

_____

_____

preceded

My afternoon music lesson **preceded** my evening volleyball game.

If you preceded a friend to class, who arrived first?

_____

_____

principal

One of the **principal** ingredients in bread is flour.

What is the principal ingredient in your favorite food?

_____

_____

promote

Many zoos today **promote** the idea of animal conservation.

What idea do you think is important to promote?

_____

_____

Build Your Word List Pick a word you found interesting in the selection you read. Then use a thesaurus to create a list of synonyms and antonyms for the word. Write these synonyms and antonyms in your writer's notebook.

restrict

Parents sometimes **restrict** the amount of time their children spend watching television.

Why might parents restrict the amount of time children watch television?

_____

_____

_____

speculation

Cloudy skies lead to **speculation** over the chance of rain.

What speculation might happen in a detective story?

_____

_____

_____

withstood

The treehouse **withstood** the strong winds.

How are the meanings of _withstood_ and _survived_ similar?

_____

_____

_____

Greek and Latin Prefixes

Knowing the meanings of prefixes that come from Greek and Latin, such as _en-_ ("in," "into"), _pro-_ ("in front"), and _re-_ ("back," "again") can help you define unfamiliar words.

🔍 FIND TEXT EVIDENCE

I am not sure of the meaning of the word encourage _on page 101 of "The Democracy Debate." If I know that the prefix_ en- _means "in" or "into," I can figure out that_ encourage _means "to put courage into."_

And speculation . . . included worries that he would en|courage young students to pick up his radical ideas.

Your Turn Use Greek and Latin prefixes to help you find the meanings of these words from "The Democracy Debate."

protected (_-tect_ means "cover"), _page 102_ _____

_____

reflect (_-flect_ means "bend"), _page 103_ _____

_____

Ocean/Corbis

Ask and Answer Questions

Asking and answering questions about key details in an expository text can help you monitor, or check, your comprehension and better understand the information. Ask yourself questions as you reread each section of "The Democracy Debate."

 **FIND TEXT EVIDENCE**

When a text includes headings, use them to ask yourself a question before reading each section. If you can answer your question easily, continue on. If not, reread the section.

> Page 101
>
> ### Great Minds
>
> The word *philosopher* means "lover of wisdom," a person who seeks knowledge and is able to make good and fair decisions. One of the best-known Greek philosophers, Socrates, lived nearly 2,500 years ago. He valued wisdom highly, and he thought deeply about democracy. Socrates was one of the principal critics of government run by the people. He felt that only fair and wise individuals should be allowed to decide things.

Before reading "Great Minds," I asked, "Whose great mind is the author referring to?" While reading, I learned about Socrates, a well-known Greek philosopher who lived nearly 2,500 years ago. He had ideas about democracy and was a critic of government run by the people.

COLLABORATE

Your Turn Use the heading "The Debate Continues" on page 103 to ask a question about the section. Then answer the question, rereading as needed.

_____

_____

_____

Charts and Diagrams

The selection "The Democracy Debate" is an expository text. An expository text gives facts, examples, and explanations about a topic. It may include text features, such as headings to organize information and diagrams or charts to present information visually.

 FIND TEXT EVIDENCE

"The Democracy Debate" presents different views held by various thinkers from the past. The diagram on page 102 provides me with a visual representation of one idea. The chart on page 103 shows information from the text in a simple, organized way.

Page 103

Philosopher	Place	Time Period	Ideas About Democracy
Socrates	Greece	469-399 B.C.	Only wise and just people should govern.
Plato	Greece	427-347 B.C.	Rule should be shared by philosopher-kings, soldiers, and providers of goods.
Aristotle	Greece	384-322 B.C.	Educated and common people should each have a role in government.
Cicero	Rome	106-43 B.C.	The Roman republic—a monarch, an aristocracy, and the people—is best.

The Debate Continues

The founders of the United States also thought about how a democracy should be organized. They studied governments that had **preceded** ours and believed that the **foundation** of any new government should revisit Greek and Roman ideas. For example, Thomas Paine wrote booklets to **promote** the idea that people should govern themselves. James Madison admired Aristotle's and Cicero's beliefs in balancing power among different groups.

In 1787, Madison helped Alexander Hamilton write a set of essays called *The Federalist* to encourage states to ratify the Constitution. They made the case for having a *pair* of law-making groups. The smaller Senate would be similar to Rome's senate, while the House of Representatives would give more people a voice. They also endorsed having one president and a system of courts to interpret the laws.

Today, people are still debating what the meaning of *democracy* is and how our government should be organized. The U.S. Constitution has been amended more than 25 times to reflect changing ideas. Yet it is important to remember that our government has roots in ideas from ancient times. Democracy has **withstood** the test of time.

Summarize

Use your notes, the diagram, and the chart to write a summary of the different ideas people have had about democracy over the centuries.

Charts

Charts often summarize information or compare related details from the text.

Diagrams

Diagrams illustrate specific ideas from the text in a more visual way.

 COLLABORATE

Your Turn Explain what information you learn from the diagram and chart on pages 102–103 of "The Democracy Debate."

_____

_____

_____

_____

Compare and Contrast

Authors of expository texts sometimes organize their ideas by comparing and contrasting them. A text about history often presents differing views that people had about a topic.

🔍 **FIND TEXT EVIDENCE**

When I reread "The Democracy Debate," I can look for the ways the author compares and contrasts the ideas that ancient philosophers had about government. Signal words and phrases, such as "unlike" and "agreed with," help me identify how the philosophers' ideas were similar and how they were different.

Socrates
believed that only wise people should govern

Both
believed that common people should not govern by themselves

Plato
believed philosopher-kings should govern with soldiers and common people

Your Turn Reread "The Democracy Debate." Compare and contrast Plato's and Aristotle's ideas about government. Use the graphic organizer to help you organize the information.

Ocean/Corbis

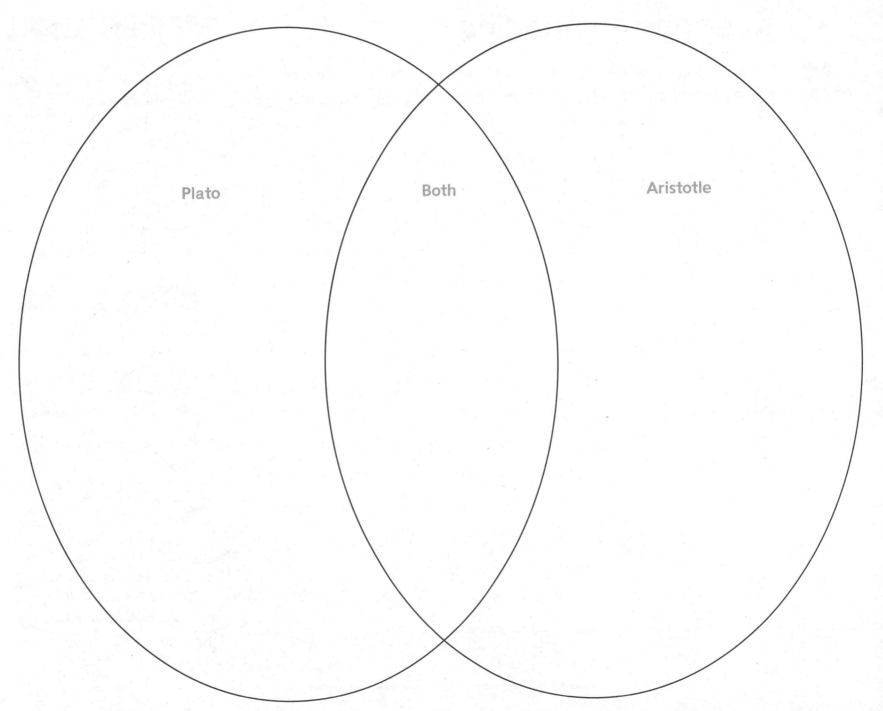

Plato

Both

Aristotle

Respond to Reading

COLLABORATE

Discuss the prompt below. Think about how the author organizes the information about democracy. Use your notes and graphic organizer.

How does the author help you understand how views about democracy have changed over time?

_____

_____

_____

_____

_____

_____

_____

_____

_____

_____

_____

_____

Grammar Connections

Check your writing for comma splices. A comma splice happens when only a comma joins two independent clauses into one sentence. For example: *Plato formed a school called the Academy, a star pupil there was Aristotle.* To fix the comma splice, separate the two clauses: *Plato formed a school called the Academy. A star pupil there was Aristotle.*

Identify and Gather Information

Before you research a topic, you need to choose your focus. You may need to narrow your focus to more easily identify relevant sources. When you **identify and gather relevant information** from a variety of sources

- think about the purpose of your research and what questions you hope to answer;
- make an outline or list main ideas to focus your research;
- take notes on the information you need;
- keep track of the sources you used.

What would you do if you were having difficulty identifying relevant information?

_____

_____

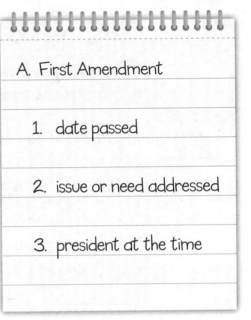

A. First Amendment

1. date passed

2. issue or need addressed

3. president at the time

The outline above shows the categories one student will keep in mind to help focus her research about each amendment.

Make a Slideshow Work with a group to choose three amendments to the United States Constitution. Check with the other groups to make sure you have chosen different amendments. Then create a slideshow to present information about each amendment. Use these questions as you identify and gather relevant information:

- What is the purpose of the amendment?
- When was the amendment passed?
- Why was the amendment necessary?

Plan how you can present your information in the most interesting way. After you complete your slideshow, you will present it to your class.

Who Created Democracy?

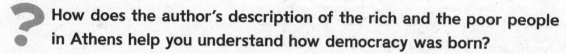 How does the author's description of the rich and the poor people in Athens help you understand how democracy was born?

Literature Anthology: pages 98–107

COLLABORATE

Talk About It Reread the first four paragraphs on **Literature Anthology** page 100. Talk with a partner about the differences between the rich and the poor people in Athens.

Cite Text Evidence What words and phrases does the author use to compare the people of Athens? Record evidence in the chart and tell why it is important.

Make Inferences

To determine why descriptions of the people of Athens are important, consider what the descriptions tell you about people's feelings and motivations. What can you infer about how the rich and the poor felt about their places in society?

The Rich	The Poor	Why It's Important

Write The author's description of both rich and poor people helps me

understand how democracy was born by _____

_____

How does the author's use of idioms help you visualize the conflicts in Athens and the American colonies?

COLLABORATE

Talk About It Reread **Literature Anthology** page 102. Talk with a partner about the conflicts in ancient Athens and the American colonies.

Cite Text Evidence What idioms does the author use? Write them and explain them. Tell how they all help you visualize conflict.

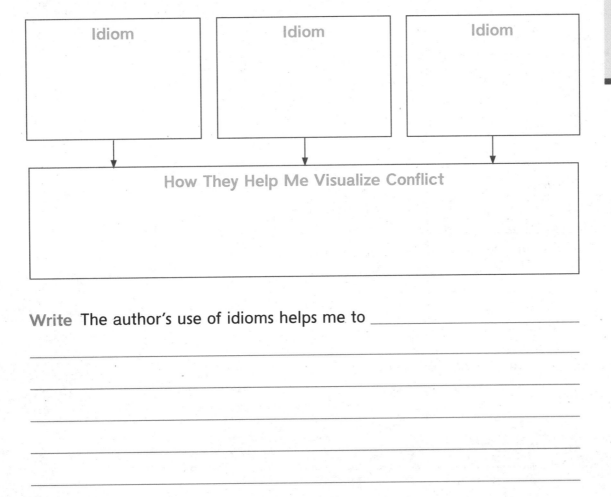

Idiom	Idiom	Idiom

How They Help Me Visualize Conflict

Write The author's use of idioms helps me to _____

_____

_____

_____

_____

? **Why does the author use transitional phrases?**

Talk About It Reread **Literature Anthology** page 106. Talk with a partner about how transitional phrases help you understand the events at the Constitutional Convention.

Cite Text Evidence What transitional phrases does the author use, and how do they help you? Write text evidence here.

Transitional Phrases	Author's Purpose

Write The author uses transitional phrases to _____

_____

_____

Respond to Reading

Discuss the prompt below. Think about what you've read about the development of democracy. Use your notes and graphic organizer.

Think about how Connie Nordhielm Wooldridge organizes information in this selection. How do her choices help you understand the development of democracy?

_____

_____

_____

_____

_____

_____

_____

_____

_____

_____

_____

Quick Tip

Use these sentence starters to talk about and cite text evidence.

Connie Nordhielm Wooldridge compares and contrasts . . .

She also uses transitional phrases . . .

She wants me to understand . . .

Self-Selected Reading

Choose a text and fill in your writer's notebook with the title, author, and genre of your selection. Include a personal response to the text in your writer's notebook. A personal response might include an experience you had that is similar to what you read. It might also include how you feel about what you are reading.

How Ideas Become Laws

Literature Anthology:
pages 110–111

Democracy in Action

[1]   National laws apply to everyone in the United States, while state and local laws are for people who live in a particular state or city. Almost anyone can suggest a law.

[2]   Steve and his dad contacted Marta Ortiz, who was a member of the state assembly. Along with representatives in the state senate, assembly members make laws. After speaking with Steve, Ms. Ortiz agreed that bicycle helmets were an important safety issue, so she said she would propose and sponsor a bill, or a plan for a law.

An Idea Becomes a Law

[3]   During a committee hearing with assembly members, Steve and Ms. Ortiz explained why they felt the law was necessary. The committee rewrote the bill to include only people younger than 18 years of age, and then it passed it on to the assembly. The assembly and the senate approved it, and   the governor signed it!

Reread paragraph 1. **Circle** what the author says about who can suggest laws.

Write it here:

_____

COLLABORATE

Reread paragraphs 2 and 3. Talk with a partner about the steps Steve and his dad take to try to get his idea to become a law.

In the margin, **number** the steps it took for Steve's idea to become a law.

A Law Takes Shape

Ms. Ortiz displayed the following chart to show Steve the process a bill takes to become a law in their state.

Step 1: The bill goes to a clerk, who reads the bill to the state assembly.

⬇

Step 2: The bill goes to a committee. If the committee approves the bill, it goes to the full state assembly.

⬇

Step 3: Representatives debate the bill then vote on it. If it passes in the assembly, it goes to the state senate.

⬇

Step 4: A state senate committee votes on the bill. If it passes, the full senate debates the bill then votes on it. If it is approved, it goes to the governor.

⬇

Step 5: The governor can sign the bill into law, do nothing so that it automatically becomes law after 5 to 14 days, or veto it. A veto means the law is rejected. Most state assemblies and senates can override a veto by a two-thirds majority vote.

Reread the flowchart. **Circle** the reason Ms. Ortiz showed this chart to Steve.

COLLABORATE

Reread Steps 1–5. Talk with a partner about who has a say in whether or not a bill becomes a law. **Underline** the text evidence and write who has a say here:

_____

_____

_____

_____

Why is "A Law Takes Shape" a good title for this flowchart? Use text evidence and write your answer here:

_____

_____

_____

_____

? **How does the flowchart help you understand the process Steve and his father went through to have an idea become law?**

Talk About It Reread the flowchart on page 117. Talk about what you learn from the information in the flowchart.

Cite Text Evidence How do the steps in "A Law Takes Shape" connect with the steps Steve and his dad took? Write them in this chart.

Main Text	Flowchart

Write The author uses a flowchart so I can see _____

_____

_____

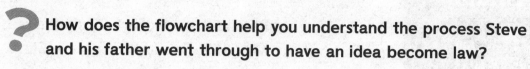

Synthesize Information

Combining the information in the main text with information in a text feature can often help you draw a conclusion about an idea important to the topic. Think about what you learned. What can you conclude about how difficult it is to turn an idea into a law?

D. Hurst/Alamy

Author's Purpose

An author's purpose is the main reason he or she writes something. Most authors write to persuade, inform, or entertain. When you read a text, think about what the author wants the readers to know and why the author wants them to know this.

FIND TEXT EVIDENCE

In the flowchart from "How Ideas Become Laws" on page 117, the author lists the steps it takes for a bill to become a state law. Listing the steps in order helps the author explain the process clearly to readers.

> **Step 1:** The bill goes to a clerk, who reads the bill to the state assembly.
>
> **Step 2:** The bill goes to a committee. If the committee approves the bill, it goes to the full state assembly.

Your Turn Reread the section "A Rocky Ride" in "How Ideas Become Laws" on page 110 of the **Literature Anthology**.

- What is the author's purpose for including this story about Steve?

  _____

  _____

- How does the author accomplish his or her purpose? _____

  _____

  _____

Remember that you can have more than one purpose for writing. For example, you might want to inform readers about a topic in a way that is entertaining, or you might want to convince readers as well as inform them. Your specific purpose or purposes will likely affect the tone, word choice, and focus of your piece.

Text Connections

? How do the photographer and the authors of *Who Created Democracy?* and "How Ideas Become Laws" help you understand democracy?

Quick Tip

How does the photograph reflect the idea that democracy means "government by the people"?

Talk About It Look at the photograph and read the caption. Talk to a partner about what you see in the photograph. Focus on where the people are and what they are doing.

Cite Text Evidence **Circle** clues that show how people are participating in democracy. Think about why their actions are important.

Write The photographer and the authors

help me understand democracy by _____

_____

_____

_____

_____

_____

_____

_____

_____

This picture shows people voting at a polling place. A polling place is where voters cast, or give, their votes during an election.

Present Your Work

Discuss how you will present your slideshow about your chosen amendments to the U.S. Constitution. Use the Presenting Checklist as you and your classmates share your slideshow presentations. Discuss the sentence starters below and write your answers.

One thing that surprised me about the amendments is _____

_____

_____

_____

_____

I would like to know more about _____

_____

_____

_____

Sixty-sixth Congress of the United States of America;

At the First Session,

Begun and held at the City of Washington on Monday, the nineteenth day of May, one thousand nine hundred and nineteen.

———

JOINT RESOLUTION

Proposing an amendment to the Constitution extending the right of suffrage to women.

———

Resolved by the Senate and House of Representatives of the United States of America in Congress assembled (two-thirds of each House concurring therein), That the following article is proposed as an amendment to the Constitution, which shall be valid to all intents and purposes as part of the Constitution when ratified by the legislatures of three-fourths of the several States.

"ARTICLE———

"The right of citizens of the United States to vote shall not be denied or abridged by the United States or by any State on account of sex.

"Congress shall have power to enforce this article by appropriate legislation."

Speaker of the House of Representatives.

Vice President of the United States and President of the Senate.

Tech Tip

Prior to presenting your slideshow, make sure each slide can be read from the back of the classroom. If not, ask your teacher if it is possible to project the slideshow on a screen or over a whiteboard.

Presenting Checklist

- ☐ Rehearse your presentation in front of another person. Ask for feedback.
- ☐ Speak slowly, clearly, and with appropriate volume and pronunciation.
- ☐ Emphasize points so that the audience can follow important ideas.
- ☐ Make eye contact with the audience. Do not just look at your slideshow.
- ☐ Listen carefully to questions from the audience.
- ☐ Use formal language in your presentation.

National Archives and Records Administration

Literature Anthology:
pages 98–107

Expert Model

Features of an Expository Essay

An expository essay explains a topic by presenting a clear central, or main, idea followed by supporting information. An expository essay

- introduces the topic in a way that grabs readers' interest;

- supports the topic and main ideas with relevant facts, quotations, and supporting details organized in a purposeful way;

- uses transition words and phrases to connect ideas.

Word Wise

As Connie Nordhielm Wooldridge introduces her topic on page 99, she uses the pronoun *we* to describe herself and her readers. This creates a supportive and inviting tone by giving readers the impression that the writer will be with them as they dive into the topic.

Analyze an Expert Model Studying expository texts will help you learn how to write one of your own. Reread page 99 of *Who Created Democracy?* in the **Literature Anthology.** Write your answers to the questions below.

How does the author capture the reader's interest in the first paragraph? __

_____

_____

_____

What details does the author use to explain the meaning of "democracy"?

_____

_____

_____

Plan: Choose Your Topic

Brainstorm With a partner, talk about different forms, or types, of government throughout history. If you need ideas about different forms of government, research the topic online or in books. On a sheet of paper, make a list of the types of government and something you know or would like to know about each one.

Writing Prompt Choose one form of government from your list to research further. Then write an expository essay that tells about that form of government.

I will research and write about _____.

Purpose and Audience Think about who will read or hear your expository essay. Will your purpose be to inform, persuade, or entertain? Then think about the language you will use to write your essay. Will it be formal or informal? Why?

My purpose is to _____.

My audience will be _____.

I will use _____ language when I write my expository essay.

Plan In your writer's notebook, make a Main Idea and Details chart to plan your expository essay. Fill in the Main Idea box with a statement about the form of government you will discuss.

Quick Tip

To help you choose a topic, identify a specific time period and place that interests you. Think about a movie you saw or a book you read that was about that time period. What type of government was in place? What do you want to learn about the government? What do you want others to learn?

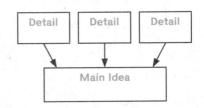

Plan: Focus on a Topic

Narrowing a Topic Once you have chosen the form of government, decide what aspects, or features, of that government you will focus on. Choose a specific location and time period and ask questions about what you most want to know. For example, depending on the form of government, you might ask how, when, and why that government was formed. Keep your questions in mind as you research information in print and online sources. As you plan your first draft, ask the following questions:

- Have I done enough research related specifically to my topic?

- Am I including only facts and details that give information about the main ideas?

- Will this information help me explain my topic clearly?

List three details you will include in your expository essay.

 _____

 _____

 _____

 Take Notes As you research, add information to your Main Idea and Details chart. Keep track of your sources so that you can refer to them again, and so that you will be able to cite them later.

Digital Tools

For more information about online searching, watch "Search with Keywords." Go to **my.mheducation.com**.

Draft

Supporting Details Authors use details from their research to support their main ideas. Supporting details may include facts, definitions, quotations from experts, and examples. In the excerpt from "The Democracy Debate" below, the author supports the topic of democracy by introducing a famous philosopher and discussing his ideas.

> One of the best-known Greek philosophers, Socrates, lived nearly 2,500 years ago. He valued wisdom highly, and he thought deeply about democracy. Socrates was one of the principal critics of government run by the people. He felt that only fair and wise individuals should be allowed to decide things.

Now use the excerpt as a model to write a paragraph about your topic. Focus on a specific idea relevant to your topic. Support your central idea with relevant details from your research.

_____

_____

_____

_____

Write a Draft Use your Main Idea and Details graphic organizer to help you write your draft in your writer's notebook. Remember to include accurate information and to cite the sources of your facts and details.

Grammar Connections

As you write your draft, be careful not to use any run-on sentences. A run-on sentence incorrectly combines two sentences. Break run-on sentences into two sentences or add a comma and a conjunction. For example: *A monarchy is one form of government a king or queen is the ruler.* This can be rewritten as: *A monarchy is one form of government. In a monarchy, a king or queen is the ruler.*

Revise

Transitions Effective writers revise their drafts to make sure their ideas connect in a clear and natural way. Transition words like *also, for instance, since, yet,* and *consequently* can be used to link ideas with details and with other ideas in your essay. Read the sample paragraph below. Then revise it by adding transition words and phrases to show more clearly how the ideas are connected.

> The United States Constitution was signed on September 17, 1787.
> It has been amended more than 25 times to reflect changing ideas.
> It is important to remember our government has roots in ideas from ancient times.

_____

_____

_____

_____

Quick Tip

As you choose transition words and phrases, think about the relationship between the ideas.

- To show different ideas, use these transitions: *yet, however, on the other hand.*

- To show sequence or chronology, try *originally, a century later, after nearly two decades, today.*

- To introduce additional information, use *furthermore, also, in addition.*

Remember to add a comma after transition words or phrases that introduce a sentence.

 Revision Revise your draft and check that all your facts and ideas are relevant to your topic and are presented in a logical order. Add appropriate transitions to show a sequence of events, compare or contrast ideas, or introduce additional information.

Peer Conferences

Review a Draft Listen carefully as a partner reads his or her work aloud. Take notes about what you liked and what was difficult to follow. Begin by telling what you liked about the draft. Ask questions that will help the writer think more about the writing. Make suggestions that you think will make the writing stronger. Use these sentence starters.

I enjoyed this part of your draft because . . .

To clarify this idea, you could add supporting details that . . .

I have a question about . . .

I wasn't sure how the idea of . . . connected to . . .

Partner Feedback After your partner gives you feedback on your draft, write one of the suggestions that you will use in your revision. Refer to the rubric on page 129 as you give feedback.

Based on my partner's feedback, I will _____

_____

After you finish giving each other feedback, reflect on the peer conference. What was helpful? What might you do differently next time?

Revision As you revise your draft, use the Revising Checklist to help you figure out what text you may need to move, elaborate on, or delete. Remember to use the rubric on page 129 to help you with your revision.

Revising Checklist

- [ ] Do I consistently use language appropriate for my topic and audience?
- [ ] Do I need to add more details to better support my topic and ideas?
- [ ] Do I need to delete any details to make this section more focused on the topic?
- [ ] Do I use enough transition words to connect ideas?

Tech Tip

Use software that tracks changes as you review your partner's work. Then work together to review each other's suggestions. Look at and accept or reject each change one by one, rather than accepting all the changes at once. Finally, before you save your work, briefly discuss how the revisions improved your writing.

Edit and Proofread

When you **edit** and **proofread** your writing, you look for and correct mistakes in spelling, punctuation, capitalization, and grammar. Reading through a revised draft multiple times can help you make sure you're correcting any errors. Use the checklist below to edit your sentences.

Grammar Connections

When you proofread your essay, make sure that you have capitalized all the proper nouns. Capitalize historic events, periods of time, documents, and nationalities.

✔ Editing Checklist

☐ Are there any run-on sentences or sentence fragments?

☐ Do all sentences have subject–verb agreement?

☐ Are proper nouns, including abbreviations and acronyms, capitalized?

☐ Are introductory transition words and phrases followed by a comma?

☐ Are plural nouns used correctly?

☐ Are all words spelled correctly?

List two mistakes you found as you proofread your essay.

1 _____

_____

_____

2 _____

_____

_____

Publish, Present, and Evaluate

Publishing When you **publish** your writing, you create a clean, neat final copy that is free of mistakes. As you write, be sure to print neatly. Leave the space of a pencil point between letters and the space of a pencil between words. Consider adding illustrations, photos, or maps to help readers better understand the information in your essay.

Presentation When you are ready to **present** your work, rehearse your presentation. Use the Presenting Checklist to help you.

Evaluate After you publish your writing, use the rubric below to **evaluate** your writing.

What did you do successfully? _____

What needs more work? _____

_____

✔ **Presenting Checklist**

☐ Speak clearly and loudly enough so your audience can hear you.

☐ Slow your pace by pausing after introducing new or difficult information.

☐ Enunciate new or difficult words or names.

☐ Display any visuals so that everyone can see them.

☐ Answer questions thoughtfully, using specific details from your essay.

4	3	2	1
• gives an informative, interesting, and detailed explanation of a topic using a clear main idea • includes many supporting details gathered from research to inform readers • includes a variety of transitions to connect ideas and clarify the relationships between them	• informs readers about a topic using a clear main idea • includes some supporting details gathered from research to inform readers • uses some transitions to connect ideas	• makes an effort to inform, but the main idea is unclear • includes few supporting details based on research to inform readers • uses few transitions to connect ideas	• does not state a main idea about the topic • does not include any supporting details to inform readers • does not use transitions to connect ideas

Talk About It

This fresco, or wall painting, is from a town in ancient Rome. Think about what the people in the painting might have been like. How might the woman and the girl be related? Both are dressed up. Are they celebrating a special occasion? The woman is playing a kind of harp called a *kithara*. What does her expression show? How does she feel about performing?

Talk to a partner about what you see in the fresco. Discuss what it tells you about the everyday lives of the ancient Romans. Fill in the web with examples.

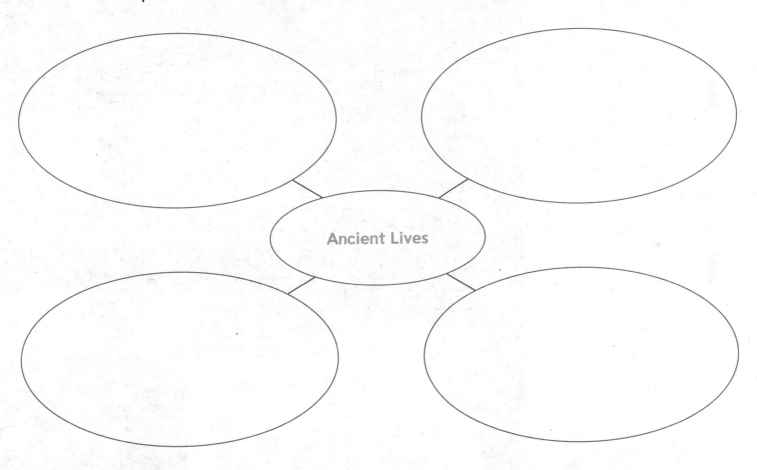

Ancient Lives

 Go online to **my.mheducation.com** and read the "Ancient Comforts" Blast. Think about conveniences we take for granted today. How did people in ancient times contribute to the development of those conveniences? Blast back your response.

TAKE NOTES

Before you read, preview the story by asking questions about the title, subheads, and illustrations. Write your questions below. Then look for answers to your questions as you read the story.

_____

_____

_____

As you read, take note of

Interesting Words _____

_____

_____

_____

Key Details _____

_____

_____

_____

_____

Yaskul's Mighty Trade

Essential Question

?

What was life like for people in ancient cultures?

Read about the importance of trade along the Silk Road in the ancient Kushan Empire.

Winston Trang

Located in what is now Afghanistan, the ancient city of Bactra in the Kushan Empire was a key market for merchants traveling the Silk Road trade route. In A.D. 110, lively commerce attracted merchants from east and west to the famous market in Bactra. In the following, Yaskul, the 12-year-old son of a Bactrian merchant, is eager to make his first official trade.

I Make Plans

It is early, but I am awake. Though we are only in the month of *Hyperberetaios*, it is a cold autumn day. As I quickly dress, I think about how the Chinese caravan arrived last night. If winter comes early, we may not see another caravan for months, as snow will close the passes. My family must have success at the market tomorrow.

Tomorrow I become a trader, I think. Father says I will be there only to watch and learn, but Grandfather says that Father is too cautious. He says Father makes timid trades and does not obtain the best prices, especially for lapis lazuli.

Lapis lazuli! How I love the brilliant blue stone that comes from the mines up north. Grandfather says that even the Egyptians prized this stone. He has awarded me some beads of my own and is instructing me on how to price them. "You listen, and you learn from me. Always watch the eyes of the man you bargain with. The eyes say when he is willing to pay more and when he will walk away."

Thieves!

When Grandfather and I reach our storage room today, Father is already there. "Thieves!" he cries. "They took everything!" Grandfather surveys the room and says it is not everything. I too spot yarn and metal cups tossed on the floor.

FIND TEXT EVIDENCE

Read

Introduction–Paragraph 1
Setting

Underline details that give information about the setting.

Paragraphs 2–3
Point of View

Who is telling the story?

_____

_____

Paragraph 4
Make Predictions

How do you think the characters will react to the theft? Explain your answer.

_____

_____

_____

Reread

Author's Craft

How does the illustration on page 132 help you understand the story?

FIND TEXT EVIDENCE 🔍

Read

Paragraph 1

Connotations and Denotations

Does *common* give a negative or positive feeling? **Underline** clues that help you decide.

_____

_____

Paragraphs 2–7

Make Predictions

Predict whether Yaskul's trade will be successful or unsuccessful. **Circle** text supporting your prediction.

_____

_____

Reread

Author's Craft

Why do you think the author has Yaskul and Zhang meet?

Father points to a small **alcove**, a shelf we have carved in the wall. "The thieves missed our wool rugs and sacks of salt. But all our lazuli stones are gone!" I comprehend how little is left for the market tomorrow. What remains are **domestic** items, and common home goods will not fetch many *drachm* coins. The merchants from China will likely dismiss our wares. Quickly, I remind Father that I still have my lazuli beads.

Grandfather peers at me, thinking. "Yes," he says, nodding. "Your stones are now of the **utmost** importance, our only hope for a successful trade. You must convince the Chinese that your stones are of the highest quality, or we will not get the best price."

I swallow hard. Grandfather smiles and puts his hand on my shoulder. "Don't fret, Yaskul. You possess the skill to make this trade a mighty one."

I Make a Friend

In the evening, I slip away to observe the Chinese traders before we meet them at market. I feel my eyes widen when the traders draw close to their fire's light. Their **exotic** robes truly glow with color. They are so much finer than my clothes.

Suddenly, one man of perhaps 19 years walks toward me. I jump back, but he smiles and waves at me. "Do not be frightened." His voice is friendly. "Is Bactra your home?" I am amazed that he is so **fluent** in my language. This young man has traveled much already, I think. "Are you a trader?" he asks me.

"I am Yaskul," I say. "My family are traders." He introduces himself as Zhang. "I have heard that name," I answer. "Did not a great man named Zhang come to Bactra long ago?"

Zhang nods. "Zhang Qian was sent to find allies for us. But he found instead your marvelous marketplace. He called your people 'shrewd traders.'"

(bkgd) Winson Trang; (tl) Liu Xiaofeng/TAO Images Limited/Alamy Stock Photo; (tc) PASCAL PAVANI/AFP/Getty Images; (tcl) I. Rozenbaum & F. Cirou/PhotoAlto; (tcr) AsiaStock/Fotosearch Value/Getty Images; (tr) Stockbyte; (b) PjrStudio/Alamy

We smile. I tell him of the **upheaval** caused today by the theft of our goods. "Your luck was hard. Even so, you will trade well," Zhang says. I hope he is right.

Market Day

I have strung my beads as a necklace, which shows the stones well. Father has guarded our remaining merchandise all night. With Grandfather, we transport it to the marketplace. Today's bright sun will make the stalls grow hot and **stifling**.

I am amazed by all the goods for sale: tea, almonds, elegant ceramics, carved ivory and jade, and the finest Chinese silk. We reach our stall as the Chinese traders arrive. Zhang nods to me as Father begins bartering with the oldest Chinese merchant, but this elder does not seem impressed by our offerings.

Then Zhang speaks. "Do you have any of the vivid blue stones your people are known for?" Grandfather gently pushes me forward. Nervously, I hold out my necklace. I notice the oldest merchant's eyes light up, and I hear myself tell him how particularly fine these beads are. The trading grows lively, and before I realize it, we agree on a high price. I hand him the necklace, and Father collects a handful of *drachms*.

Zhang winks at me, but says not a word. After the Chinese traders depart, Grandfather embraces me, and even Father thumps me on the back. Now I can truly call myself a trader!

Summarize

Use your notes to orally summarize the story. Be sure to include only the most important details about the key events and to describe them in a logical order, from beginning to middle to end.

FIND TEXT EVIDENCE

Read

Paragraphs 1–5
Point of View

Underline Yaskul's description of the older merchant's reaction to the necklace. Why does Yaskul respond the way he does?

_____

_____

_____

_____

Reread

Author's Craft

Why do you think the author chose to have Yaskul narrate the story rather than an outside narrator?

Fluency

Take turns reading "Market Day" with a partner. Discuss punctuation that helped you read expressively.

Vocabulary

Use the example sentences to talk with a partner about each word. Then answer the questions.

alcove

We moved the table into the **alcove** in our kitchen.

What might you find in a classroom alcove?

_____

_____

commerce

Commerce involves exchanging money for goods and services.

What kinds of commerce are you familiar with?

_____

_____

Build Your Word List Pick a word you found interesting in the selection you read. Use a word web to write different forms of the word. An online or a print dictionary can help you find related words.

domestic

The brothers' **domestic** chores include cleaning up after meals.

What are some domestic chores that you do?

_____

_____

exotic

The zoo has many **exotic** animals from around the world.

What are some exotic animals you might find at a zoo?

_____

_____

fluent

Carmen is **fluent** in both English and Spanish.

Who is likely to be fluent in more than one language?

_____

_____

stifling

Air conditioning keeps a building cool in **stifling** heat.

What might you do on a stifling hot day?

_____

_____

_____

upheaval

An energetic new puppy may cause **upheaval** in a home.

How might a puppy cause upheaval?

_____

_____

_____

utmost

A good doctor treats patients with the **utmost** care.

What is a synonym for utmost?

_____

_____

_____

Connotations and Denotations

Denotation is a word's literal meaning as explained in a dictionary. **Connotation** is the feeling or idea associated with a word. This can be identified by looking to the context in which a word appears.

FIND TEXT EVIDENCE

On page 133, Grandfather views Father's trades as cautious and timid. Both words have similar meanings, or denotations. The connotation of timid is negative, as in "always fearful." Cautious may also have a negative connotation, as in "being overly careful."

. . . Grandfather says that Father is too cautious. He says Father makes timid trades . . .

Your Turn Decide whether the connotation of each word from "Yaskul's Mighty Trade" is more positive or negative.

tossed, *page 133* _____

little, *page 134* _____

shrewd, *page 134* _____

Make Predictions

Pausing occasionally to **predict** what will happen next in a text can improve a reader's understanding of the plot and keep the reader involved in the story. As you read "Yaskul's Mighty Trade," identify clues in the text that help you **confirm** or **revise** your predictions.

🔍 FIND TEXT EVIDENCE

You may have wondered how the theft of the lazuli stones would affect Yaskul. Reread the first two paragraphs of "Thieves!" on pages 133 and 134.

Page 134

Father points to a small alcove, a shelf we have carved in the wall. "The thieves missed our wool rugs and sacks of salt. But all our lazuli stones are gone!" I comprehend how little is left for the market tomorrow. What remains are domestic items, and common home goods will not fetch many drachm coins. The merchants from China will likely dismiss our wares. Quickly, I remind Father that I still have my lazuli beads.

I read that Yaskul's beads are the only lazuli stones the family has left. From this I predicted that Yaskul would help his family. When I read that Yaskul would trade the beads himself, it confirmed my prediction.

Your Turn Explain one prediction you made about the role Zhang would play in Yaskul's trade. Was your prediction correct? If not, tell how you revised it.

_____

_____

_____

Setting and Foreign Language Words

"Yaskul's Mighty Trade" is historical fiction. Historical fiction takes place in a real setting from history and may refer to real people from the past. It may also include foreign words that reflect the narrative's setting.

FIND TEXT EVIDENCE

I can tell "Yaskul's Mighty Trade" is historical fiction because the story takes place in a real city in the past. The characters mention a real person from history. Words from other languages, such as drachms, *show that the characters live in a foreign place.*

Page 134

Father points to a small **alcove**, a shelf we have carved in the wall. "The thieves missed our wool rugs and sacks of salt. But all our lazuli stones are gone!" I comprehend how little is left for the market tomorrow. What remains are **domestic** items, and common home goods will not fetch many *drachm* coins. The merchants from China will likely dismiss our wares. Quickly, I remind Father that I still have my lazuli beads.

Grandfather peers at me, thinking. "Yes," he says, nodding. "Your stones are now of the **utmost** importance, our only hope for a successful trade. You must convince the Chinese that your stones are of the highest quality, or we will not get the best price."

I swallow hard. Grandfather smiles and puts his hand on my shoulder. "Don't fret, Yaskul. You possess the skill to make this trade a mighty one."

I Make a Friend

In the evening, I slip away to observe the Chinese traders before we meet them at market. I feel my eyes widen when the traders draw close to their fire's light. Their **exotic** robes truly glow with color. They are so much finer than my clothes.

Suddenly, one man of perhaps 19 years walks toward me. I jump back, but he smiles and waves at me. "Do not be frightened." His voice is friendly. "Is Bactra your home?" I am amazed that he is so **fluent** in my language. This young man has traveled much already, I think. "Are you a trader?" he asks me.

"I am Yaskul," I say. "My family are traders." He introduces himself as Zhang. "I have heard that name," I answer. "Did not a great man named Zhang come to Bactra long ago?"

Zhang nods. "Zhang Qian was sent to find allies for us. But he found instead your marvelous marketplace. He called your people 'shrewd traders.'"

Historical Setting

The setting places the plot in a real place from the past.

Foreign Language Words

The characters use ancient words from another language.

Your Turn Find additional evidence that indicates "Yaskul's Mighty Trade" is historical fiction. Explain how these details impact the setting or the plot.

_____

_____

_____

_____

Point of View

In fiction, a narrator tells the story. When one of the story's characters is the narrator, the story has a first-person point of view. When the narrator is someone outside the story, that story has a third-person point of view. In third-person limited point of view, the narrator knows the thoughts and feelings of only one character. In third-person omniscient, or all-knowing, the narrator knows the thoughts and feelings of every character.

A first-person narrator can only state his or her own thoughts about other characters in a story. Look beyond the narrator's opinions for details that indicate that the narrator might be wrong about another character's traits or motivations.

 FIND TEXT EVIDENCE

When I reread "I Make Plans" on page 133, I see that the narrator uses the first-person pronouns I, me, *and* my. *This shows that the story is narrated by a character in the story. I know I will learn about other characters and events from only the narrator's perspective.*

Details		Point of View
Yaskul is the narrator. He uses the pronouns "I," "me," and "my" to tell the story.		The story has a first-person point of view.
Yaskul describes what Father and Grandfather tell him.		

 Your Turn Reread "Yaskul's Mighty Trade." Decide what you can and can't know about the characters and events. List the information in the graphic organizer. Tell how you know the story has a first-person point of view.

Details	Point of View
Yaskul is the narrator. He uses the pronouns "I," "me," and "my" to tell the story.	The story has a first-person point of view.
Yaskul describes what Father and Grandfather tell him.	

..

Respond to Reading

COLLABORATE

Discuss the prompt below. Think about the setting and historical details the author includes. Use your notes and graphic organizer.

How does the author help readers understand the historical importance of trade to people in the Kushan Empire?

_____

_____

_____

_____

_____

_____

_____

_____

_____

_____

_____

_____

_____

Quick Tip

Use these sentence starters to discuss the text and to organize ideas.

- *The illustration and introduction help . . .*
- *The setting shows . . .*
- *The first-person narration makes it clear that . . .*

Grammar Connections

As you write, check that any pronouns you use have a clear antecedent. For example: *The merchant agreed to the price Yaskul set and paid* him *in drachms*. The pronoun *him* refers back to Yaskul and not to the merchant.

Relevant Information

Information that is **relevant** is directly connected to the topic you are researching. To help you identify information relevant to your topic, follow the tips listed below.

- Focus your topic by writing a sentence or question that states the purpose of your research.
- Develop a list of keywords that directly relate to your topic.
- Use multiple print and digital sources to locate information.

How might you use a list of keywords to find relevant information in an

informational print book? _____

_____

_____

In ancient Egyptian civilization, a scribe learned to read and write.

COLLABORATE

Create a Journal Entry With a partner or in a group, research an ancient civilization. Study elements of everyday life at that time. Then use your imagination to write a journal entry of someone from that civilization. You might write from the point of view of a ruler, a teacher, a laborer, or any other citizen. Include answers to the questions below.

- What is a typical day like for this citizen?
- What does the citizen do, and how is his or her role important to the civilization?
- How does the person feel about his or her position, or status?

Discuss what print and digital sources you might use in your research. Remember to write from a first-person point of view using pronouns, such as *I, me,* and *my.*

Tech Tip

Make sure to put quotation marks before and after specific phrases in online searches. This will ensure that the search engine identifies the specific phrase and not just the individual words within the phrase.

Roman Diary

Literature Anthology:
pages 112–127

How do the illustrations and captions help you understand more about Iliona's and Apollo's new lives?

Talk About It Reread **Literature Anthology** pages 114–115. Review the illustrations and captions. Talk with a partner about how they add to what you read in Iliona's diary.

Cite Text Evidence What new information do you learn from the illustrations and captions? Compare it to what you read in the diary entry.

Iliona's Diary	Illustrations and Captions

Write The illustrations and captions help me understand that _____

_____

_____

Make Inferences

Details in the text and illustrations will help you infer information about the characters and how they are feeling. For example, Iliona doesn't tell readers directly that she misses Apollo. How do her words and the illustration on page 114 help you understand how she feels?

How does the author use figurative language to help you visualize what Etruscan Street was like?

Talk About It Reread the Day IV entry on **Literature Anthology** page 116. Talk with a partner about how the author describes Etruscan Street.

Cite Text Evidence How does the description of Etruscan Street help you visualize what Iliona is experiencing? Write details in the web.

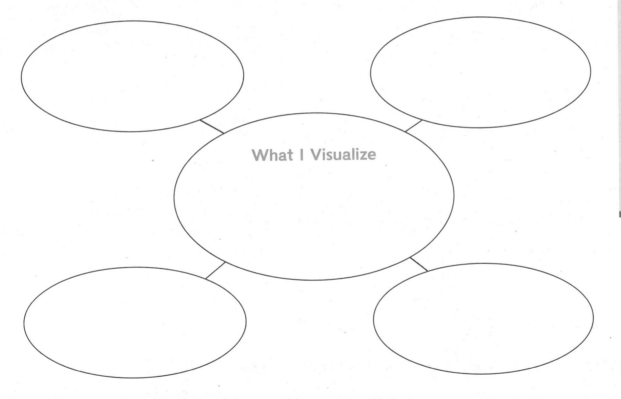

What I Visualize

Quick Tip

Figurative language refers to words that are used in a different way than their usual, or literal, meaning. One example of figurative language in *Roman Diary* is the description of thieves as people who "will skin you alive and sell you back your own hide." This doesn't mean the thieves will hurt Iliona. It means the thieves are so good at stealing that she won't even know she has been robbed. How does this expression help you visualize Etruscan Street?

Write The author's use of figurative language helps me visualize _____

_____

_____

_____

Reread | ANCHOR TEXT

? **How does the author help you understand why Iliona saves Lydia from the fire?**

Talk About It Reread paragraphs 5–7 on **Literature Anthology** page 125. Talk about how the women respond to the fire and how it makes Iliona feel.

Cite Text Evidence What events led to Iliona's decision to save Lydia? Write text evidence in the chart.

Write The author helps me understand why Iliona saves Lydia by _____

_____

_____

Quick Tip

A diary entry expresses the writer's own thoughts and feelings. As you read the entries in Iliona's diary, think about why she includes certain details and omits others. This will give you a better understanding of how she feels and why she takes certain actions.

Respond to Reading

COLLABORATE

Discuss the prompt below. Think about how figurative language helps readers visualize a setting. Use your notes and graphic organizer.

How does Richard Platt's use of figurative language help you understand what life was like in ancient Rome?

_____

_____

_____

_____

_____

_____

_____

_____

_____

_____

_____

_____

_____

_____

_____

Quick Tip

Use these sentence starters to talk about and cite text evidence.

Richard Platt uses figurative language to . . .

His descriptions and illustrations help me see why Iliona . . .

This point is important because . . .

Self-Selected Reading

Choose a text to read independently and fill in your writer's notebook with the title, author, and genre. Record your purpose for reading. For example, you may be reading to answer a question or for entertainment.

The Genius of Roman Aqueducts

Literature Anthology:
pages 130–133

1   Did you know that many children in ancient Rome did the same thing? In fact, they played many of the same games you do, jumping rope or playing catch, and when they were thirsty they came inside for a drink or went to any number of public drinking fountains around the city.

2   Most children in Rome knew how water was transported to their city. But did you ever wonder where the water you drink comes from? Or how it got to your faucet?

3   The fact is, if you do not have a well in your own backyard, the water you use at home may come from a long distance away. However, it doesn't travel by truck or train. Water is transported to you via a complex system of connected pipes and tunnels. These pipes and tunnels channel water from reservoirs and transport it to you. We call the system that carries water an aqueduct. In Latin, this word means "a conductor of water."

Reread paragraph 1. **Circle** the ways children in ancient Rome are like children today. Write how the children are similar here:

Children in Ancient Rome	Children Today

Talk with a partner about how the author invites you to keep reading. Reread paragraph 2 and **make a mark** in the margin beside how she does that.

Reread paragraph 3. **Underline** how the author helps you understand what an aqueduct is.

1   The city of Rome was not different. It also grew up alongside a river, the Tiber, one of the longest rivers in Italy. But as Rome grew and became the capital of a large empire, it needed more water than the Tiber could provide. So how did the ancient Romans obtain and transport this water?

Aqueducts in Rome

2   The Romans didn't invent the idea of aqueducts. They had been used in Mesopotamia to supply water to crops some distance from the Tigris and Euphrates. However, the aqueducts the Romans built were far more complex than anything that had come before them. Long, long before engines had been invented that could pump water, the ancient Romans figured out how to use natural forces to do the same thing. They used the water pressure created by gravity to move water hundreds of miles. It would travel from mountaintop lakes, down the sides of mountains, across valleys and into cities and towns.

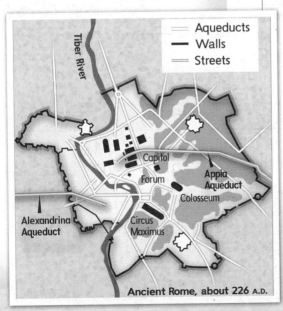

Aqueducts
Walls
Streets

Tiber River

Capitol
Forum
Appia Aqueduct
Colosseum
Alexandrina Aqueduct
Circus Maximus

Ancient Rome, about 226 A.D.

Reread paragraph 1. **Circle** the problem that arose as Rome grew. **Underline** the author's transition to the next section.

COLLABORATE

Reread paragraph 2 and look at the map. What information tells how the Romans moved water? **Make a mark** in the margin where the author provides this information. Write it here:

_____

_____

Circle clues in the map that show how water is transported into the city.

? Why is "The Genius of Roman Aqueducts" a good title for this selection?

Talk About It Reread the excerpt on page 149. Talk with a partner about how the Romans built the aqueducts.

Cite Text Evidence What clues help you see how the Roman aqueducts were "genius"? Record text evidence in the chart.

Evaluate Information

To evaluate the title "The Genius of Roman Aqueducts," look for text evidence that explains how the aqueducts were a smart, creative solution to a problem the Romans had.

Text Evidence	Why It's Important

Write "The Genius of Roman Aqueducts" is a good title because _____

_____

_____

_____

Author's Purpose

Authors have a purpose, or reason, for writing. In order to accomplish his or her purpose, an author thinks about the intended audience or reader, and then chooses words and details suited to the purpose and audience.

FIND TEXT EVIDENCE

In the first paragraph of "The Genius of Roman Aqueducts" on **Literature Anthology** page 130, the author explains what life was like for children in ancient Rome. In the next paragraph, the author asks a question and then compares what children do today with what Roman children did long ago.

> Did you know that many children in ancient Rome did the same thing? In fact, they played many of the same games you do, jumping rope or playing catch, and when they were thirsty they came inside for a drink or went to any number of public drinking fountains around the city.

Your Turn Reread the rest of Literature Anthology page 130.

COLLABORATE

- How does the author spark readers' curiosity about drinking water?

  _____

  _____

- What is the author's purpose for writing this part of the text?

  _____

  _____

Readers to Writers

When you write, make sure to keep your purpose in mind. An author's primary purpose may be to persuade, inform, or entertain. If you are writing to inform, think about what facts and details are important and interesting for readers. Consider techniques you can use, such as asking questions, to earn and keep your reader's attention.

Text Connections

? How do this cave painting, Iliona's diary in *Roman Diary,* and the aqueducts in "The Genius of Roman Aqueducts" help you understand what life was like for cultures of the past?

COLLABORATE

Talk About It Talk with a partner about what you see in the photograph of the cave painting. Focus on what is happening and what you might learn about the people who painted it.

Cite Text Evidence Look at the painting and read the caption. **Circle** clues that tell you something about how the people who created it lived.

Write The cave painting and selections I read this week help me understand about cultures of the past by

_____

_____

_____

_____

_____

_____

_____

_____

> ### Quick Tip
>
> Keep in mind that just like an author, an artist thinks carefully about the details to include in a painting. When you look at a painting, think about its overall meaning. Then identify specific details that help you understand the artist's purpose for painting.

This cave painting of a buffalo was found in France. The painting is more than 11,000 years old.

CAROLUS/age fotostock

Present Your Work

COLLABORATE

Discuss how you will present your journal entry about everyday life in an ancient civilization. Consider how audio, visuals, or even costume pieces or props might also help bring the time period to life for your audience. Use the Presenting Checklist as you practice your presentation. Discuss the sentence starters below and write your answers.

As part of my research on everyday life in an ancient culture, I discovered

_____

_____

_____

I would like to know more about _____

_____

_____

_____

Quick Tip

Practice will improve your presentation and give you the confidence to read with expression, as if you really experienced the events you are describing.

✓ **Presenting Checklist**

☐ Rehearse your presentation in front of a classmate. Ask for feedback.

☐ Use appropriate expression and intonation.

☐ Speak in a loud enough volume to be heard clearly, even in the back of the classroom.

☐ Make eye contact with the audience.

☐ Answer questions thoughtfully using details from your research.

Calaimage/Robert Daly/Getty Images

Talk About It

COLLABORATE

The people in the photograph on page 154 are visiting an ancient Greek temple in Sicily, an island in the Mediterranean Sea. Take a moment to contemplate what people may have been thinking when they built this temple some 2,400 years ago. What can you learn from something that has survived for so many years?

Look at the photograph. Talk with a partner about what you see. Discuss what you can learn about the past from ancient structures and other objects from history. Fill in the chart with examples.

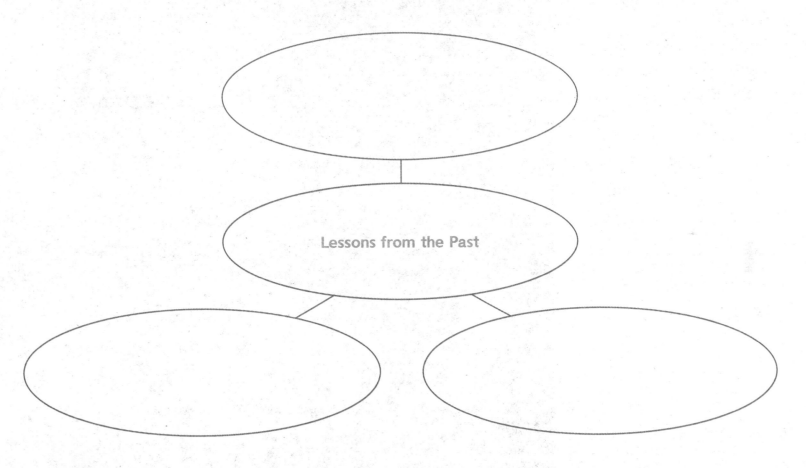

Lessons from the Past

BLAST BACK!
studysync

Go online to **my.mheducation.com** and read the "Phillis Wheatley, Child Poet" Blast. Think about why it is important to read works written in past times? What can these texts help us understand? Then blast back your response.

Marc Schlossman/Photographer's Choice/Getty Images

TAKE NOTES

Making and confirming predictions can help you focus on the text and monitor your understanding. Read the titles of each poem and review details in the photo and illustration. Predict what each poem will be about and write your predictions below. As you read, see if you can confirm your predictions or if you need to revise them.

_____

_____

_____

As you read, take note of

Interesting Words _____

_____

_____

Key Details _____

_____

_____

_____

_____

(bkgd) De Agostini Picture Library/De Agostini/Getty Images; (c) Chris Deeney/Alamy Stock Photo

Essential Question

?

What can the past teach us?

Read how two poets experience the past and what they learn from it.

Ozymandias

I met a traveler from an antique land

Who said: "Two vast and trunkless legs of stone

Stand in the desert . . . Near them, on the sand,

Half sunk, a shattered visage lies, whose frown,

And wrinkled lip, and sneer of cold command,

Tell that its sculptor well those passions read

Which yet survive, stamped on these lifeless things,

The hand that mocked them, and the heart that fed:

And on the pedestal these words appear:

'My name is Ozymandias, king of kings:

Look on my works, ye Mighty, and despair!'

Nothing beside remains. Round the decay

Of that colossal wreck, boundless and bare

The lone and level sands stretch far away."

—Percy Bysshe Shelley

FIND TEXT EVIDENCE

Read

Page 157

Sonnet and Lyric Poetry

How many lines are in the poem, and how many syllables per line?

_____

_____

Whose thoughts and feelings does the poem share? How do you know?

_____

_____

Theme

Underline details that tell what happened to the statue. What message do these details convey?

_____

_____

Reread

Author's Craft

How do the details of the statue and setting help the poet show how things change over time?

FIND TEXT EVIDENCE

Read

Page 158

Rhyme Scheme and Meter

Read the first stanza aloud. Where do you hear rhyme?

_____

_____

_____

Personification

Underline text in stanza 3 that gives human actions to something nonhuman. What does this tell you about the speaker's feelings?

_____

_____

_____

Reread

Author's Craft

How does the poet use vivid language to help you understand the speaker's affection for books and the printing press?

Lifelong Friends

When I was but a lad of ten,

I joined the world of working men,

Apprentice was the name I took,

I learned the way to print a book.

The print shop had an air of gloom,

And sunlight seemed to shun the room,

My master was a man I feared,

He raged at me and pulled his beard.

The printing press was friend to me,

Majestic as a mighty tree,

And so I grew to love that place,

My heart would sing, my pulse would race.

Each time I worked with type and ink,

I always trembled just to think

That all those many rows of words

Would soon fly up and out like birds.

Those books were tutors glad to share

Their words with people everywhere,

So many books for eager hands,

For rich and poor in many lands.

Though now my youth has passed away,

And near the hearth I spend my day,

When I'm forlorn, I contemplate

The many books I helped create.

As I commemorate my past,

One view of mine will always last:

Each book a lifelong friend might be

To someone, yes, but most to me.

—Constance Andrea Keremes

Make Connections

Explain how reflecting on the past could have an influence on you in the present. Talk about whether your predictions on page 156 were confirmed.

FIND TEXT EVIDENCE

Read

Page 159

Lyric Poetry

Circle a detail about the speaker's feelings in the fourth stanza. What does this detail help you understand?

_____

_____

_____

_____

Theme

Underline what the speaker does when he feels forlorn. What is the message about life the poet wants to communicate?

_____

_____

Reread

Author's Craft

Why do you think the poet chose the title "Lifelong Friends"?

Vocabulary

Use the example sentences to talk with a partner about each word. Then answer the questions.

commemorate

Our town holds a parade to **commemorate** the Fourth of July.

How do you commemorate Thanksgiving Day?

_____

_____

contemplate

I had to **contemplate** the problem before I was able to solve it.

What decision have you had to contemplate?

_____

_____

forlorn

I felt **forlorn** when my best friend moved away.

What is a synonym for forlorn?

_____

_____

majestic

The snow-capped mountains looked **majestic** in the distance.

What is a synonym for majestic?

_____

_____

Poetry Terms

lyric poetry

I like reading **lyric poetry** because it expresses the poet's strong personal feelings.

What might the topic of a lyric poem be?

_____

_____

sonnet

Each of the 14 lines in a **sonnet** contains pairs of stressed and unstressed syllables.

Do you think a sonnet might be easy or hard to write? Why?

_____

_____

rhyme scheme

A poem's **rhyme scheme** is the pattern made by its end rhymes.

Why must you read an entire poem to identify its rhyme scheme?

_____

_____

_____

meter

Meter is the pattern of stressed and unstressed syllables in a poem.

How could you determine a poem's meter?

_____

_____

_____

Build Your Word List Reread "Ozymandias" on page 157. Choose three interesting words from the poem and write them in your writer's notebook. Then use a print or online thesaurus to find two synonyms for each word. Write the synonyms next to the words.

Personification

Personification is figurative language that gives human qualities to nonhuman objects, animals, or ideas. Personification can make a poem more vivid by creating an image in the reader's mind.

🔍 FIND TEXT EVIDENCE

In the line And sunlight seemed to shun the room, *the poet gives a human ability to the sunlight. This personification of sunlight gives me a mental image of sunlight purposely avoiding the room, and it emphasizes the darkness of the setting.*

The print shop had an air of gloom,
And sunlight seemed to shun the room,
My master was a man I feared,
He raged at me and pulled his beard.

Your Turn Find another example of personification in "Lifelong Friends." Tell how it helps you understand an idea the poet is using figurative language to convey.

_____

_____

_____

Rhyme Scheme and Meter

Quick Tip

Words rhyme when they have the same ending sound, but that doesn't mean they end with the same spelling. To hear and identify rhyming words, read the poem aloud. Doing this will also help you hear and recognize the meter.

Poets often use sound patterns to write a poem's **stanzas,** or groups of lines. This can give a poem a musical quality. One sound pattern, **rhyme scheme,** is the pattern of rhyming words at the end of each line. Another pattern, **meter,** is the arrangement of stressed and unstressed syllables. A stressed syllable is the accented, or emphasized, syllable in a word. In the word *apple*, the first syllable is stressed and the second is unstressed.

 FIND TEXT EVIDENCE

Reread "Lifelong Friends" on pages 158–159. Listen for rhyming patterns and patterns of stressed and unstressed syllables.

Page 158

When I was but a lad of ten,
I joined the world of working men,
Apprentice was the name I took,
I learned the way to print a book.

The last words in each pair of lines rhyme. If I use letters to represent this pattern, each stanza has a rhyme scheme of AABB. Each line has four pairs of syllables. The first syllable in each pair is unstressed, and the second is stressed.

Your Turn Reread "Ozymandias" on page 157. Use letters to represent the rhyme scheme in lines 11–14. Then tell whether the pattern of stressed and unstressed syllables is the same or different in each line.

_____

_____

_____

Sonnet and Lyric Poetry

Lyric poetry expresses a speaker's personal thoughts and feelings. Although it has a musical quality, it does not always rhyme.

A **sonnet** is a type of lyric poem with fourteen lines and a pattern to its end rhymes. It often contains pairs of stressed and unstressed syllables.

FIND TEXT EVIDENCE

The speaker in "Ozymandias" describes a reaction to a ruined statue. When I read the poem aloud, it sounds almost like a song, so I think it's a lyric poem. It has fourteen lines, a pattern of rhyming words, and a pattern of stressed and unstressed syllables in each line. This structure tells me it's also a sonnet.

Page 157

Ozymandias

I met a traveler from an antique land
Who said: "Two vast and trunkless legs of stone
Stand in the desert . . . Near them, on the sand,
Half sunk, a shattered visage lies, whose frown,
And wrinkled lip, and sneer of cold command,
Tell that its sculptor well those passions read
Which yet survive, stamped on these lifeless things,
The hand that mocked them, and the heart that fed:
And on the pedestal these words appear:
'My name is Ozymandias, king of kings:
Look on my works, ye Mighty, and despair!'
Nothing beside remains. Round the decay
Of that colossal wreck, boundless and bare
The lone and level sands stretch far away."

—Percy Bysshe Shelley

Rhyming words may be at the ends of every other line.

Your Turn Reread "Lifelong Friends" on pages 158–159. Decide if it is an example of a lyric poem. Then determine if it is a sonnet. Explain why.

COLLABORATE

Theme

The theme of a poem is the overall idea or message that the poet wants to communicate to readers. Sometimes a poem can have more than one theme. To determine a theme of a poem, look for key details that provide clues about the message the poet wants to convey.

 **FIND TEXT EVIDENCE**

In "Lifelong Friends," the speaker describes the "gloom" of the print shop and how his master "raged." Yet he loves making books for people with the "majestic" printing press. I can look for more details about this contradiction to infer the poet's message and identify its theme.

Detail
"The print shop had an air of gloom"

↓

Detail
"My master was a man I feared"

↓

Detail
"When I'm forlorn, I contemplate The many books I helped create."

↓

Theme
Challenging work can be fulfilling.

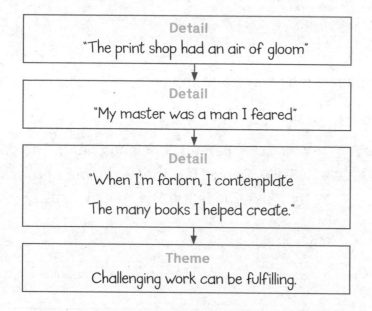

Your Turn Reread "Ozymandias" on page 157. Identify key details and record them in the graphic organizer on page 165. Use the details to determine the theme of the poem.

Paying careful attention to the language in a poem can help you identify the poem's theme. For example, repeated phrases or recurring images are clues that can help you understand the poem's message.

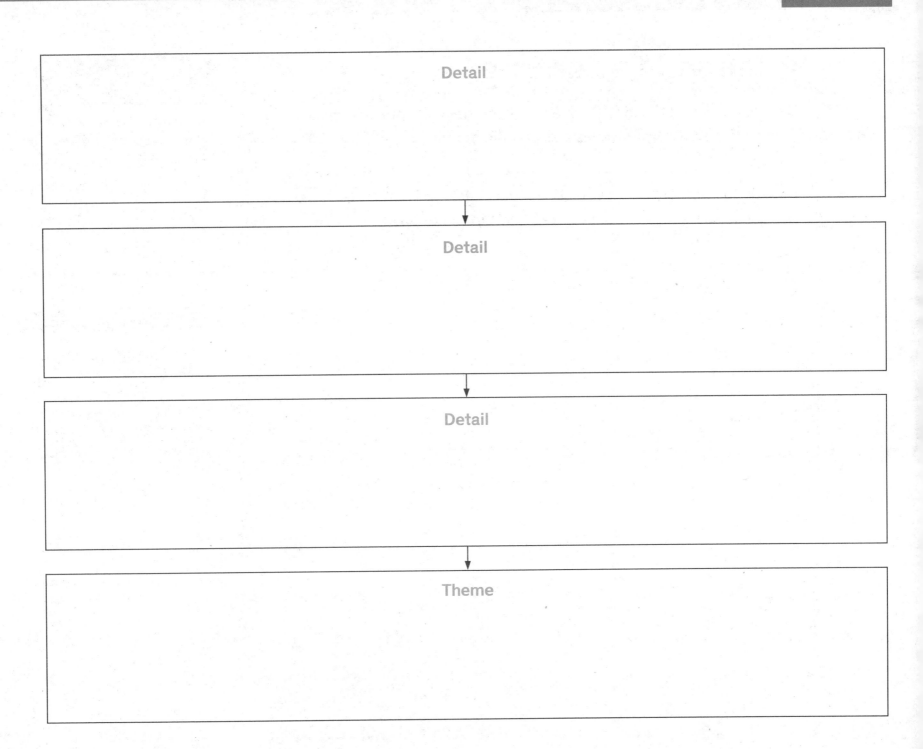

Detail

Detail

Detail

Theme

Respond to Reading

Discuss the prompt below. Think about how the poets present ideas about the past. Use your notes and graphic organizer.

How do the authors of "Ozymandias" and "Lifelong Friends" use objects to communicate ideas about our relationship to the past?

_____
_____
_____
_____
_____
_____
_____
_____
_____
_____
_____
_____
_____
_____

Evaluate Sources

When researching a topic, **evaluate** your sources to make sure they are reliable, or trustworthy. Established newspapers, book publishers, and websites for libraries, museums, universities, and governments are usually considered sources of reliable information. To evaluate a source, ask yourself these questions:

- Is the source current?
- Is the information consistent with other sources I've found?
- Does the source present information without bias, or opinion?

Why might bias make a source unreliable?

_____

_____

_____

These statues, called moai, were built hundreds of years ago by the Rapa Nui people on Easter Island in Polynesia. Name two sources you might evaluate to learn more about the statues.

_____

_____

_____

_____

COLLABORATE

Make an Educational Booklet With a partner or group, create an educational booklet about an important archaeological artifact. Include visuals as well as information. Consider these questions when deciding on a topic:

- What is the archaeological artifact, and where is it located?
- Who found it, and when was it found?
- What is its current condition?
- Why is it important or significant?

Discuss sources you could use in your research. Create a separate bibliography for your sources. You will be sharing your booklet with your classmates.

Tech Tip

Narrow your search for reliable websites by looking for sites that end in *.edu* (for school and university sites), *.gov* (for government sites), and *.org* (for sites belonging to museums and other nonprofit organizations).

Slavado/500px Prime/Getty Images

Majestic

? How does the poet use sensory language to describe the demise of the hotel and its role in history?

Literature Anthology: pages 134–136

Talk About It Reread **Literature Anthology** page 135. Talk with a partner about what happened to the hotel and what it's like now.

Cite Text Evidence What words and phrases does the poet use to describe to the old hotel? Write them in the web.

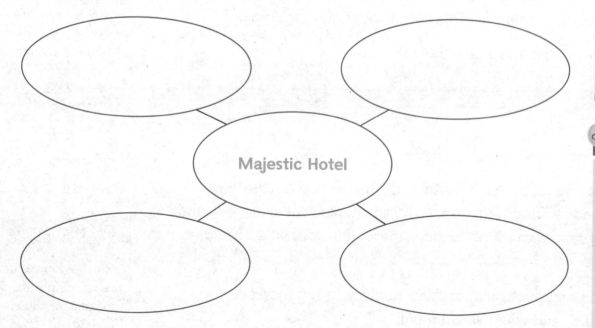

Majestic Hotel

Write The poet's use of sensory language helps me see that the hotel

_____

_____

Quick Tip

Sensory language refers to words and phrases that appeal to a reader's five senses. As you reread the poem, look for language that helps you imagine how the hotel might look, sound, or feel.

 Make Inferences

Pay attention to details that indicate time and place, such as "When gold ran out the miners laid in wait" and "slowed the westward drift." What do they help you infer about the historical significance of the hotel and the people who once stayed there?

Mummy and Clay

? How does the author of each poem help you understand the theme, or message, these poems happen to have in common?

Talk About It Reread "Mummy" and "Clay" on **Literature Anthology** page 136. Talk with a partner about what the two poems have in common.

Cite Text Evidence How do the poets help you understand the message behind their poems? Write text evidence in the chart.

Mummy	Clay

Write The poets help me see the common theme in their poems by

_____

_____

Respond to Reading

COLLABORATE

Discuss the prompt below. Apply your own knowledge of how a poet communicates a theme in a poem. Use your notes and graphic organizer.

Think about how each poet uses objects to tell about the past. How does that help you understand how they feel?

_____

_____

_____

_____

_____

_____

_____

_____

_____

_____

_____

_____

_____

_____

Quick Tip

Use these sentence starters to talk about and cite text evidence.

• *The poets use the hotel, the mummy, and clay to . . .*

• *This tells me . . .*

• *I can see that the poets think the past . . .*

Self-Selected Reading

Connecting what you are reading to what you already know helps you learn. Choose a text and write its title, author, and genre in your writer's notebook. As you read, make connections to personal experiences or to other texts you've read. Write your ideas in your notebook.

Maestro and Tradition

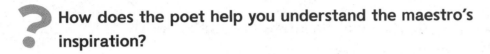

? **How does the poet help you understand the maestro's inspiration?**

Literature Anthology:
pages 138–139

Talk About It Reread "Maestro" on **Literature Anthology** page 138. Talk with a partner about the way the poet describes how the maestro's past influences his present.

Cite Text Evidence What phrases does the poet use to describe the maestro's inspiration? Write them in the web.

Quick Tip

Think about the meanings of the words *inspiration* and *influence*. Both describe an effect someone or something has on a person's thinking or actions.

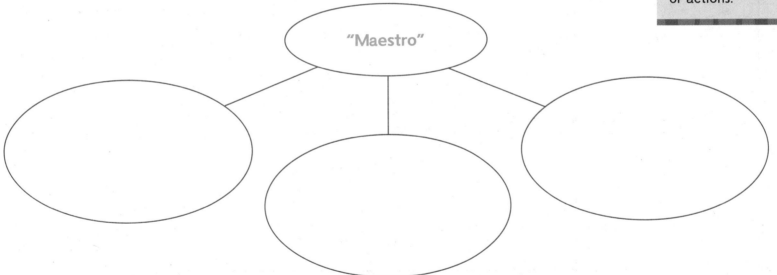

"Maestro"

Write The poet helps me understand the maestro's past influences by

_____

_____

_____

? How do the poets use point of view to set the tone in their poems?

Talk About It Reread "Maestro" and "Tradition" on **Literature Anthology** pages 138–139. With a partner, identify the speaker's point of view in each poem and describe how it affects the tone of each poem.

Cite Text Evidence What words and phrases help you understand who is speaking and how it affects tone? Write text evidence in the chart.

"Maestro"	"Tradition"	Tone

Write The poets set tone by using point of view to _____

_____

_____

_____

In poetry, tone refers to the speaker's attitude or feeling toward a subject. For example, a poem's tone may be respectful, cheerful, resentful, or cautionary. You can identify a poem's tone by looking for how the poem's language and sound devices reveal the speaker's feelings.

Word Choice

Poets choose the words they use very carefully. They often use sensory language, or words that appeal to the reader's senses. Sensory language adds meaning and emotion to a poem by helping the reader visualize objects, actions, or ideas.

FIND TEXT EVIDENCE

In "Maestro" on **Literature Anthology** page 138, the speaker describes the Mexican songs he and his father used to play. In the final lines, the speaker uses phrases such as "pure note" and "sweet on the tongue" to appeal to the reader's sense of taste. This helps the reader understand how satisfying and pleasant the music is for the speaker.

Your Turn Reread "Tradition" on **Literature Anthology** page 139.

- How does the choice of words in the first four lines help you visualize the speaker's actions? _____

  _____

  _____

- Find another example of sensory language in "Tradition." What does this help you understand? _____

  _____

  _____

  _____

Library of Congress Prints and Photographs Division [LC-DIG-ppmsc-00343]

Text Connections

How is the way the photographer shows the archaeologist similar to the way the poets use artifacts as inspiration in the poems "Majestic," "Mummy," and "Clay"?

Talk About It Look at the photograph and read the caption. Talk with a partner about what each person is doing.

Cite Text Evidence **Circle** clues in the photograph that help you understand how the archaeologist and the student feel about the bones they are examining. **Underline** one clue in the caption that shows how you know the archaeologist is interested in what she does.

Write I know that artifacts and objects from the past can inspire because they _____

_____

_____

_____

_____

_____

_____

Quick Tip

A photographer, like a poet, captures emotion by focusing on details that reveal how people are feeling. As you compare the photo to the poems, look for details that show that the archaeologist and the student are interested in the bones.

An archaeologist shows a skull to a student. The bones are from a museum's storage collection.

Expression and Phrasing

When you read a poem aloud, think about its meaning and look for words that express feeling. That will help you read with **expression**, making the poem more interesting and easier to understand. Commas, colons, semicolons, periods, and other punctuation marks indicate **phrasing**, or when to pause while reading. Reading with good expression and phrasing, or prosody, can also clarify the poem's meaning.

Page 159

As I commemorate my past,
One view of mine will always last:
Each book a lifelong friend might be
To someone, yes, but most to me.

The commas and colon in this poem signal places to pause while reading.

COLLABORATE

Your Turn Turn back to pages 158 and 159. Take turns reading aloud "Lifelong Friends" with a partner. Pay attention to punctuation. Visualize what is happening in the poem. How does the poet want you to feel? Express the speaker's feelings in the way you read the poem.

Afterward, think about how you did. Complete these sentences.

I remembered to _____

_____

Next time, I will _____

_____

Expert Model

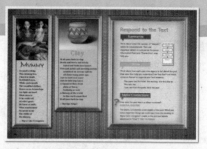

Literature Anthology: page 136

Features of a Lyric Poem

Lyric poetry expresses a speaker's thoughts and personal feelings about a topic. A lyric poem

- can include rhyme, meter, and other sound devices;

- uses sensory language, or words and phrases that appeal to a reader's senses, to help readers visualize the content of the poem;

- includes carefully chosen words that convey a certain mood.

Word Wise

Notice that "Mummy" contains only two sentences broken across several lines. The short, clipped lines help to emphasize certain ideas or images.

Analyze an Expert Model Studying lyric poems will help you learn how to plan and write your own lyric poem. **Reread** "Mummy" on **Literature Anthology** page 136. Write your answers to the questions below.

How does the speaker feel about the mummy? Explain your answer. _____

_____

_____

How does the poet use sensory language to help readers visualize the

subject of the poem? _____

_____

_____

_____

Plan: Choose Your Topic

COLLABORATE

Brainstorm With a partner, compile a list of significant events in history, such as the signing of the U.S. Constitution, the first landing on the Moon, or an important scientific discovery. To generate ideas, discuss the questions below. Then write your ideas on a separate piece of paper.

- What impact did the event have at the time it happened?

- How did the event affect the lives of those who lived through it?

Writing Prompt Choose one of the events you brainstormed and write a lyric poem about it. Think about who the speaker of your poem will be, and the thoughts and feelings the speaker might have about the event.

I will write my lyric poem about _____.

The speaker in my lyric poem will be _____.

Purpose and Audience The speaker of your lyric poem will express thoughts and feelings about a significant historical event. Who will read or listen to your poem? Will you be writing to inform, persuade, or entertain this audience?

My audience will be _____.

I will write to _____ this audience.

Plan In your writer's notebook, make an Event graphic organizer to record your speaker's thoughts and feelings about the event, and the details and language the speaker might use to communicate those thoughts and feelings. Write your event in the center.

Quick Tip

Remember that the speaker in your poem does not have to be you. A poem's speaker is just like the narrator in a story. It can be a real person from history or a made-up character. Your speaker can even be an animal or an object.

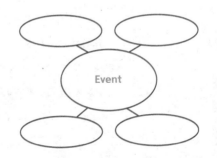

Event

Plan: Sound Devices

Rhyme Scheme and Meter Rhyme scheme and meter help give a lyric poem its musical quality. Rhyme scheme is the pattern of rhyming words at the ends of lines. Meter refers to the pattern of stressed and unstressed beats, or syllables, in a line. A stressed syllable is the accented, or emphasized, syllable in a word. In the word *winter*, the first syllable is stressed and the second is unstressed.

As you plan sound devices for your poem, ask yourself:

- Do I want to include rhyme in my poem? What interesting and relevant rhyming words might I include?

- Do I want to use meter in my poem?

- How might the musical quality of these sound devices help express the speaker's feelings?

Choose at least one sound device to use in your poem. On the lines below, write if you will use rhyme scheme, meter, or both. Also describe how you will use the sound device or devices you chose in your poem.

_____

_____

 Graphic Organizer Once you have determined how you will use sound devices in your lyric poem, fill in the rest of your Event graphic organizer. Include details about the event and the feelings you will convey. If you need more space, use a separate sheet of paper in your writer's notebook.

Draft

Sensory Language Poets often use sensory language to convey their speakers' feelings and experiences. Language that appeals to the senses helps the reader imagine the content of a poem. In the excerpt from "Lifelong Friends," look for details that appeal to your sense of sight.

> The print shop had an air of gloom,
> And sunlight seemed to shun the room,
> My master was a man I feared,
> He raged at me and pulled his beard.

Use the above excerpt as a model to write some lines with sensory language that could go in your own lyric poem. Think carefully about which of the five senses you will appeal to in your poem.

_____

_____

_____

_____

 Write a Draft Use your graphic organizer to help you write your draft in your writer's notebook. Include sensory language to describe the event and convey the speaker's thoughts and feelings. Remember to think about the sound devices you chose to include in your poem.

Revise

Word Choice When poets revise their drafts, they focus on adding precise verbs, adjectives, and adverbs that create and support a specific feeling, or mood. For example, the words in a lyric poem about the first Moon landing might create a feeling of excitement. Read the sample lines below. Then revise the lines so they contain more vivid and precise words that help support a feeling of celebration.

> We astronauts smile as we put on our heavy gear.
>
> We feel happy.
>
> We are scientists and pilots, but
>
> We feel like kids up here on the Moon.

_____

_____

_____

_____

 Revision Revise your draft. Check that you have used precise language and vivid words to create a strong feeling, or mood, in your poem that readers can respond to.

Peer Conferences

COLLABORATE

Review a Draft Listen carefully as a partner reads his or her work aloud. Take notes about what you liked and what was difficult to follow. Begin by telling what you liked about the draft. Ask questions that will help the writer think more about the writing. Make suggestions that you think will make the writing stronger. Use these sentence starters.

I enjoyed this part of your draft because . . .

More sensory language would help me understand . . .

A more precise word here might be . . .

Partner Feedback After your partner gives you feedback on your draft, write one of the suggestions that you will use in your revision. Refer to the rubric on page 183 as you give feedback.

Based on my partner's feedback, I will _____

_____

After you finish giving each other feedback, reflect on the peer conference. What was helpful? What might you do differently next time?

Revision Use the Revising Checklist and the rubric on page 183 to help you figure out what text you may need to move, elaborate on, or delete. Remember to use the rubric on page 183 to help you with your revision.

✓ Revising Checklist

☐ Does my writing fit my purpose and audience?

☐ Does my poem express the speaker's personal feelings and thoughts about the event?

☐ If I used a rhyme scheme and meter, do they create a musical quality?

☐ Have I included enough sensory language and description words?

☐ Have I included enough vivid or precise words to support the poem's mood, or feeling?

Edit and Proofread

When you **edit** and **proofread** your writing, you look for and correct mistakes in spelling, punctuation, capitalization, and grammar. Reading through a revised draft multiple times can help you make sure you're correcting any errors. Use the checklist below to edit your poem.

✓ Editing Checklist

☐ Are all proper nouns, such as names and titles, capitalized?

☐ Do all verbs agree with their subjects?

☐ Are irregular verbs used correctly?

☐ Is punctuation used correctly?

☐ Are all words spelled correctly?

Grammar Connections

Sentences in a poem may break across more than one line, but punctuation is usually still necessary to help the reader understand your language. As you edit and proofread your poem, be thoughtful about how you use punctuation.

List two mistakes you found as you proofread your lyric poem.

1 _____

_____

_____

2 _____

_____

_____

Publish, Present, and Evaluate

Publishing When you **publish** your writing, you create a clean, neat final copy that is free of mistakes. Adding visuals to your poem can make even more of an impact on your readers.

Presentation When you are ready to **present** your work, rehearse your presentation. Use the Presenting Checklist to help you.

Evaluate After you publish your writing, use the rubric below to **evaluate** your writing.

What did you do successfully? _____

What needs more work? _____

_____

4	3	2	1
• clearly expresses the speaker's feelings/ thoughts about the topic • uses sound devices that create a clear musical quality • includes sensory language to engage readers; words are chosen carefully to support the mood	• expresses the speaker's feelings/thoughts about the topic • uses sound devices that create a musical quality • includes sensory language to engage readers and words that support the mood	• expresses the speaker's feelings/thoughts, but in an unclear way • uses sound devices that create an uneven musical quality • includes some sensory language and words that support the mood	• does not express the speaker's feelings/ thoughts • uses sound devices that have no musical quality • does not include sensory language or words that support the mood

⟳ Spiral Review

You have learned new skills and strategies in Unit 2 that will help you read more critically. Now it is time to practice what you have learned.

- **Compare and Contrast**
- **Greek and Latin Prefixes**
- **Foreign Language Words**
- **Make Inferences**
- **Personification**
- **Theme**
- **Connotations and Denotations**

Connect to Content

- **Words from Other Languages**
- **"Who Owns History?"**

Read the selection and choose the best answer to each question.

The Roots of Democracy?

[1]   Democracy as we know it today is a complex topic. There are many modern democratic countries, but there is great variety in how these countries implement democratic principles. However, democracies have one thing in common: the people have a say in their government.

[2]   Many historians trace this foundational belief to ancient Greece. The word *democracy*, after all, is derived from Greek words literally meaning "rule by the people." But some scientists and researchers have argued that democratic systems predate ancient Greek civilization. They point to evidence that suggests early democratic systems existed thousands of years ago in small societies from the Mediterranean to Asia.

Democratic Systems in South Asia

[3]   The Indian subcontinent may have been one place in which early democratic systems existed. Around the 6th century B.C., various self-governing groups began to emerge in certain communities. These were assemblies of large numbers of people with much in common. They met to make decisions about important issues affecting their societies. There were many different kinds of groups with different names, and two such examples are known as *ganas* and *sanghas*.

Women cast their votes in an election at a polling station in Kashmir, India.

to resolve an important issue, it was up to the *raja*, or king, to step in and make the final decision.

5   Some researchers point to yet another early democratic system on the Indian subcontinent. A <u>panchayat</u> is a system in which residents of a village elect elders to a council. This council was then responsible for creating rules and resolving problems. *Panchayats* are still present in some locations even today.

Democratic Ideals

6   It should be stressed that these early democratic systems were not true democracies as we understand them today. In some cases, some people may have been excluded from the decision-making process. Rights that citizens of modern democracies enjoy today were not necessarily guaranteed. But these systems are notable in that they are early examples of people making decisions as a group. While authority may have been denied to some, it was not concentrated in the hands of a single ruler. Here we see kernels of democratic ideals that we can recognize in the democracy of ancient Greece, as well as in democracies around the world today.

4   *Sanghas* were assemblies of people who usually shared a common religion. No member of a *sangha* had any more power than another member, and participation in the *sangha* was encouraged so that decisions were made collectively. *Ganas* were similar to *sanghas* in that a group of people made decisions collectively. But when a *gana* could not agree on how

Anupam Nath/AP Images

SHOW WHAT YOU LEARNED

1 Based on the information in paragraph 2, you can infer that —

A the author thinks democracy is a relatively new form of government

B ancient Greek democracy had no relation to modern democracy

C the author thinks some readers will be unaware that democratic systems predated democracy in ancient Greece

D ancient Greek democracy was not very complex

Quick Tip

For multiple-choice questions, rule out the answers that are definitely wrong. Then spend some time focusing on the remaining answers.

2 In paragraph 4, a compare-and-contrast text structure helps show —

F the order in which early Indian democratic systems developed

G the reasons for the formation of different democratic systems

H problems all governing bodies encountered and how they were solved

J how two specific democratic systems worked

3 Which words help the reader understand what *panchayat* means?

A derived from Greek words literally meaning "rule by the people"

B assemblies of people who usually shared a common religion

C a group of people made decisions collectively

D system in which residents of a village elect elders to a council

4 Which word in paragraph 6 has a negative connotation, or feeling?

F stressed

G excluded

H guaranteed

J recognize

Read the poem and choose the best answer to each question.

THE CANYON

I stand atop a rugged ridge

looking through the <u>millennia</u>

at a picture of the ages,

written in 1,000 colorful layers.

5   Tangled bands of rock and mud,

and rough grits of sand and clay—

woven together,

telling the tale of past to present,

bottom to top,

10   from the beginning of time.

Once an ocean flowed here,

its seawater, salty and slick,

was filled with creatures,

like giant scallops,

15   hollow tube worms,

and curled-up snails—

some in coarse shells,

shielding them

from the rough and tumble

20   of raging storms and tides.

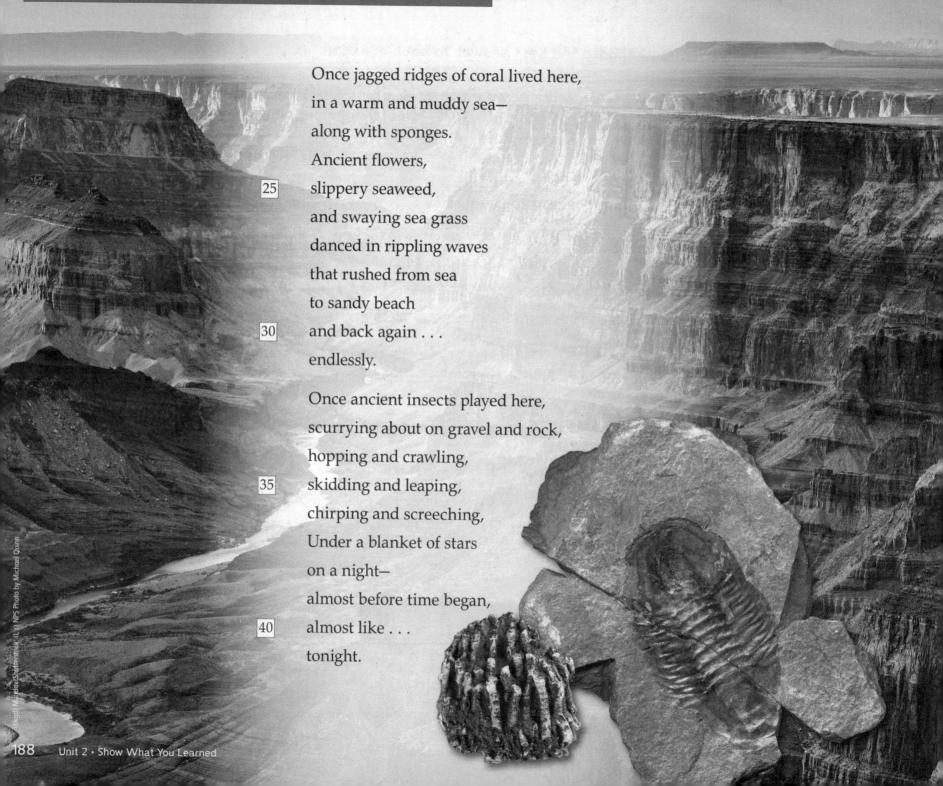

Once jagged ridges of coral lived here,

in a warm and muddy sea—

along with sponges.

Ancient flowers,

25   slippery seaweed,

and swaying sea grass

danced in rippling waves

that rushed from sea

to sandy beach

30   and back again . . .

endlessly.

Once ancient insects played here,

scurrying about on gravel and rock,

hopping and crawling,

35   skidding and leaping,

chirping and screeching,

Under a blanket of stars

on a night—

almost before time began,

40   almost like . . .

tonight.

1 The Latin prefix *mill-* means "thousand." What does <u>millennia</u> mean in line 2?

    A one thousand colors

    B one thousand feet

    C one thousand people

    D thousands of years

2 What can you infer about the poem's setting from the first stanza?

    F It is bland and colorless.

    G It is man-made.

    H It has not changed much over time.

    J It has existed for many years.

3 Which of the following lines from the poem features personification?

    A looking through the millennia

    B Once an ocean flowed here

    C Once ancient insects played here

    D Under a blanket of stars

4 Which answer choice best describes the main theme of the poem?

    F Earth's natural history spans thousands of years.

    G Landscapes rarely change.

    H There are many kinds of sea creatures.

    J It is important to take care of the environment.

Quick Tip

For multiple-choice questions, when two answers seem correct, contrast them to identify differences. Then go back to the question to see if you can choose the best answer.

EXTEND YOUR LEARNING

ONOMATOPOEIA

COLLABORATE

- Poems often feature **onomatopoeia**, or words whose sounds suggest their meanings. Read aloud these examples of onomatopoeia: *howl, swish, honk, tweet, fizz.*

- Underline examples of onomatopoeia in this stanza from a poem.

> The splash of rain against my windowpane
> Distant thunder growls
> Cozy inside, my rocker creaks

Now write your own poem on a separate paper. Include at least three examples of onomatopoeia words.

SUFFIXES

Knowing Greek and Latin suffixes can help you understand unfamiliar words.

Suffix	Meaning	Example
-ion, -tion, -sion	"the state of"	educate ⟶ education
-ous	"full of"	fame ⟶ famous
-ize	"to make"	summary ⟶ summarize

The author of *Who Created Democracy?* explains that the Stamp Act of 1765 made American colonists furious. Use the chart above to figure out the meaning of *furious.*

On a piece of paper, write and define five words using the suffixes above.

HISTORICAL AND CULTURAL SETTING

A story's **historical setting** is its time and place in history. Its **cultural setting** refers to the beliefs, traditions, and way of life of the people from this time and place. Compare and contrast life in modern-day Rome to the historical and cultural setting of *Roman Diary*.

- Research in books or online what modern Rome is like. Review *Roman Diary* to recall details about its historical and cultural setting.

- Use the Venn diagram to compare ancient and modern Rome.

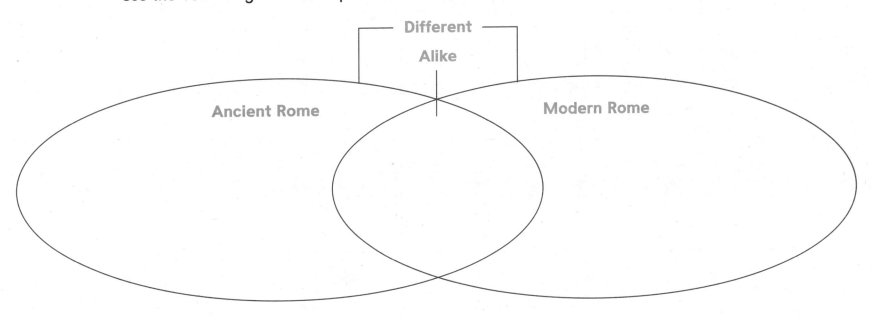

Different

Alike

Ancient Rome

Modern Rome

Now use the details you have gathered to determine how the setting of ancient Rome affected the plot of *Roman Diary*.

_____

_____

_____

WORDS FROM OTHER LANGUAGES

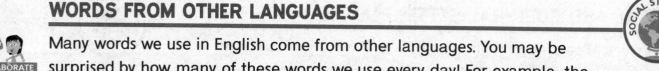

Many words we use in English come from other languages. You may be surprised by how many of these words we use every day! For example, the French language gave us the word *ballet*, while the word *kindergarten* comes from German.

Do some research to find out the meanings of the words in the chart. Also note the original language from which each word is derived.

Word We Use	Meaning	Original Language
mosquito		
rendezvous		
delicatessen		
tsunami		
piano		

Write a sentence below using one of the words from chart.

_____

_____

WHO OWNS HISTORY?

Log on to **my.mheducation.com** and reread the *Time for Kids* online article "Who Owns History?," including the information found in the interactive elements. Answer the questions below.

Who Owns History?

New laws challenge the practices of obtaining cultural artifacts.

Time for Kids: "Who Owns History?"

- What are "source nations?"

  _____

  _____

  _____

- Why do some museum professionals believe that showing antiquities outside the cultures that produced them is beneficial?

  _____

  _____

  _____

- Why do some archaeologists believe artifacts belong in their source nations?

  _____

  _____

  _____

- How might the controversy between source nations and museums be resolved?

  _____

  _____

Tom Pepeira/Iconotec/Alamy Stock Photo

TRACK YOUR PROGRESS

WHAT DID YOU LEARN?

Use the rubric to evaluate yourself on the skills you learned in this unit.
Write your scores in the boxes below.

4	3	2	1
I can successfully identify all examples of this skill.	I can identify most examples of this skill.	I can identify a few examples of this skill.	I need to work on this skill more.

☐ Compare and Contrast   ☐ Greek and Latin Prefixes   ☐ Theme

☐ Point of View   ☐ Connotations and Denotations   ☐ Personification

Something that I need to work more on is _____ because

_____

_____

_____

Text to Self Think back over the texts that you have read in this unit.
Choose one text and write a short paragraph explaining a personal
connection that you have made to the text.

I made a personal connection to _____ because _____

_____

_____

_____

_____

Present Your Work

COLLABORATE

Discuss how you will present your educational booklet with information and visuals about an important archaeological discovery. Use the Listening Checklist as your classmates give their presentations. Discuss the sentence starters below and write your answers.

An interesting fact I learned about a specific archaeological discovery is

_____

_____

_____

Now I would like to know more about _____

_____

_____

✓ Listening Checklist

☐ Listen carefully to other presenters so you can learn about the archaeological discoveries they chose.

☐ Take notes on interesting facts and details.

☐ Pay attention to how visuals illustrate the ideas presenters are communicating.

☐ Ask relevant questions and make pertinent comments at the end of the presentation.

Craigimage/Robert Daly/Getty Images